THINKING K'

MATH

Learning Fun for Growing Minds!

Grade 2

Thinking Kids™
Carson-Dellosa Publishing LLC
Greensboro, North Carolina

Thinking Kids™
Carson-Dellosa Publishing LLC
P.O. Box 35665
Greensboro, NC 27425 USA

ISBN 978-1-4838-0206-0

Table of Contents

Introduction

Welcome to *Thinking Kids™ Math!* This book contains everything you and your child need for hands-on learning and math practice. It gives you the tools to help fill knowledge gaps and build foundations that will prepare your child for higher-level math. Your child will learn to think about, know, apply, and reason with math concepts.

Thinking Kids™ Math is organized into five sections based on the skills covered. Each activity supports the Common Core State Standards and offers a fun and active approach to essential second grade math skills. Interactive lessons and the use of manipulatives build a concrete example of math concepts to help your child develop mathematical understanding.

Work through the interactive activities with your child using manipulatives around your house. Guide your child through each activity, and then allow them to perform the activity with little or no support.

Examples of common household items you could substitute for counters or blocks are different colored buttons, paper clips, pennies, and dice. A variety of manipulatives in different colors, sizes, textures, and shapes is essential to your child's learning. It is important for them to interact with different types of manipulatives so they do not associate certain concepts with certain manipulatives.

Thinking Kids™ Math promotes the use of manipulatives to engage and challenge your child. The interaction with manipulatives promotes motor skills and exploration while engaging your child in hands-on experience. Activities also call for children to draw, use tally marks, pictures, and graphic organizers. After children have worked with manipulatives, they transfer their understanding of the concept by drawing pictures in place of the manipulatives.

Each activity supports early learning standards and challenges your child's critical thinking and problem solving skills. In *Thinking Kids™ Math*, your child will learn about:

- Numbers and Operations
- Algebra
- Geometry
- Measurement
- Data Analysis and Probability

Estimate the number of counters you can pick up with one hand. Write your guess on the first line. Grab a handful of counters and put them into groups of ten. Fill in each blank. Repeat with the next bag.

Estimate: _____   Estimate: _____

I have _____ groups of   I have _____ groups of

ten and _____ left over.   ten and _____ left over.

I have _____ total counters.   I have _____ total counters.

Keeping Score

In the first row, count the balls and make tally marks for each team's goals. In the second row, count the tally marks and write scores for each game.

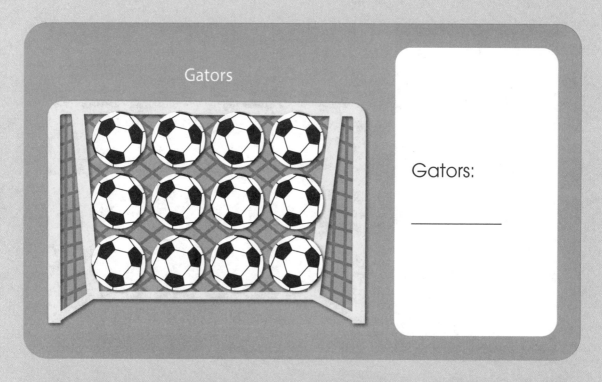

Gators

Gators:

_____

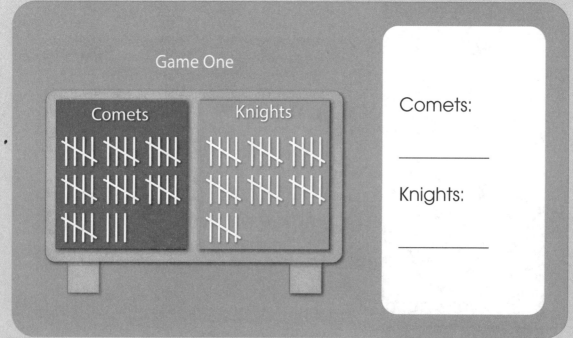

Game One

Comets   Knights

Comets:

_____

Knights:

_____

In the first row, count the balls and make tally marks for each team's goals. In the second row, count the tally marks and write scores for each game.

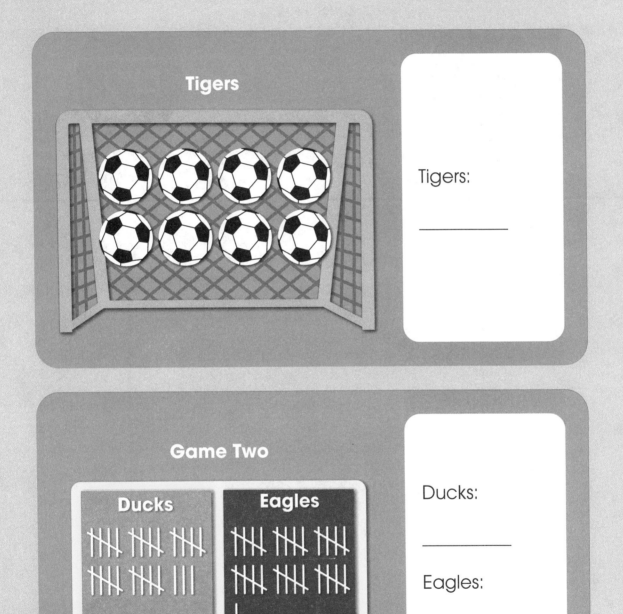

Tigers

Tigers:

_____

Game Two

Ducks   **Eagles**

Ducks:

_____

Eagles:

_____

A Number of Ways

Use base ten blocks to show each number. Draw a picture of the blocks and write the number of tens and ones in the blanks.

tens	ones

tens	ones

_____ tens 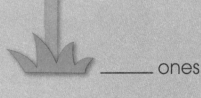 _____ ones   _____ tens _____ ones

Use base ten blocks to show each number. Draw a picture of the blocks and write the number of tens and ones in the blanks.

tens	ones

tens	ones

_____ tens   _____ ones

_____ tens   _____ ones

Expanding Numbers

Build each number with base ten blocks. Then, write each number in expanded form. The first one has been done for you.

534 = 500 + 30 + 4

27 =

301 =

876 =

984 =

Expanding Numbers

Build each number with base ten blocks. Then, write each number in expanded form.

435 =

202 =

68 =

732 =

851 =

Line Leader

Follow the directions to put the bears in order. Use counters.

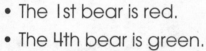

- The 1st bear is red.
- The 4th bear is green.
- The 10th bear is blue.
- The 3rd bear is yellow.
- The 2nd and 6th bears are the same color as the 10th bear.
- The 8th and 12th bears are the same color as the 4th bear.
- The 11th and 7th bears are the same color as the 3rd bear.
- The 5th and 9th bears are the same color as the 1st bear.

Monthly Math

Complete the calendar by writing the missing numbers. The first two numbers have been written for you. Write the important events below on the correct calendar days.

Piano lessons: 2nd and 3rd Saturdays

Test days: the 16th and the 23rd

Tennis practice: 1st and 4th Mondays

Dentist appointment: the 29th

September

Sunday	Monday	Tuesday	Wednesday	Thursday	Friday	Saturday
		1	2			

Monthly Math

Complete the calendar by writing the missing numbers. The first two numbers have been written for you. Write the important events below on the correct calendar days.

Piano lessons: 1st and 3rd Fridays

Test days: the 7th and the 22nd

Soccer practice: 2nd and 4th Wednesdays

Doctor appointment: the 28th

October

Sunday	Monday	Tuesday	Wednesday	Thursday	Friday	Saturday
		1	2			

Money Jars

Look at the amount of money in each jar. Draw three different bill and/or coin combinations for each amount.

$1.23

$0.78

$2.17

Thinking Kids™ Math
Grade 2

Money Jars

Look at the amount of money in each jar. Draw three different bill and/or coin combinations for each amount.

$2.33

$1.57

$0.63

Money Jars

Look at the amount of money in each jar. Draw three different bill and/or coin combinations for each amount.

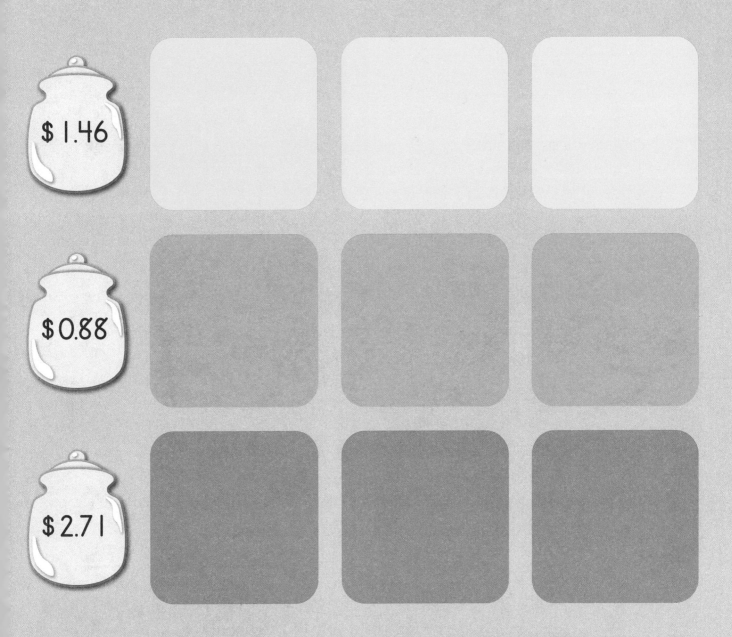

$ 1.46

$0.88

$ 2.71

Thinking Kids™ Math
Grade 2

Unlock the Code

Follow the clues to figure out the code number for each lock.

My ones digit is 6. My tens digit is 1 plus my ones digit. My hundreds digit is 1 less than my ones digit. What number am I?

My ones and hundreds digits are the same. My tens digit is 2 less than my ones digit. My ones digit is 4 + 4. What number am I?

Unlock the Code

Follow the clues to figure out the code number for each lock.

My ones digit is 4. My tens digit is 1 plus my ones digit. My hundreds digit is 1 less than my ones digit. What number am I?

My hundreds digit is 6. My ones digit is half of my hundreds digit. Add my hundreds digit and ones digit together to get my tens digit. What number am I?

Number Know How

Show the number in four different ways. Use tally marks, number words, drawings, or counters.

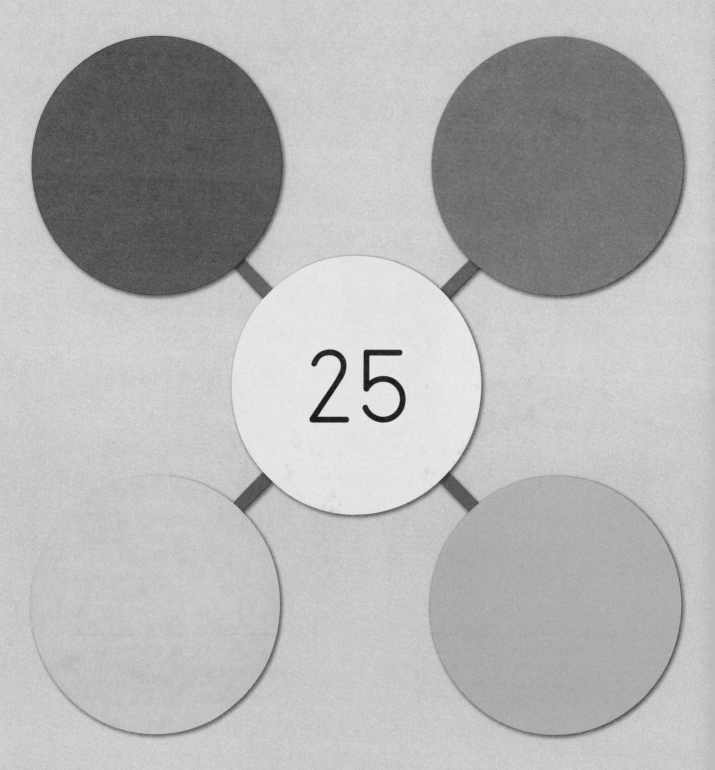

25

Show the number in four different ways. Use tally marks, number words, drawings, or counters.

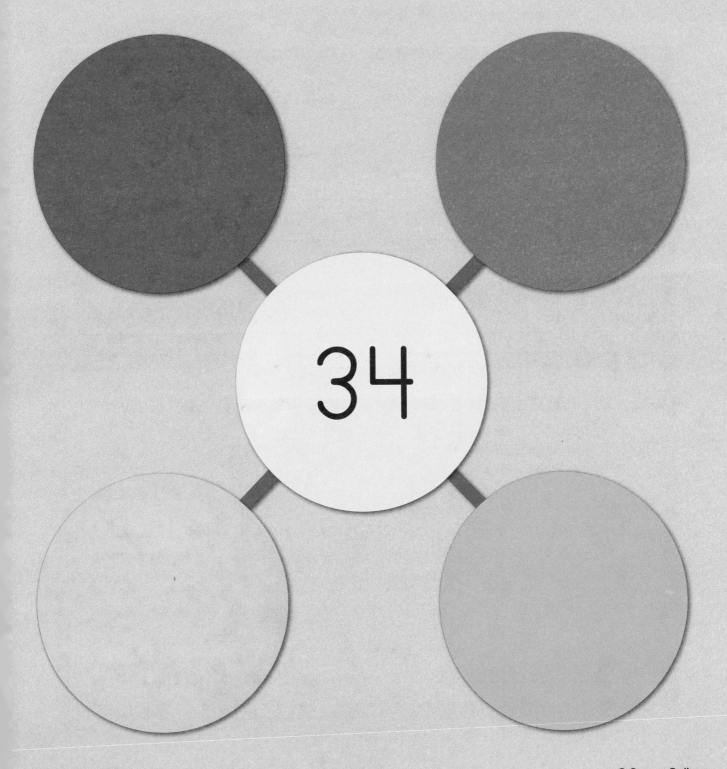

Write Me a Check!

Write the amount of each check in word form on the line.

Bailey Bug
86 Spotted Highway
Insectville, IZ 3X2Q8

1001

Pay to Lady Beetle Café

$718.00

00/100 **dollars**

For: dinner party

Bailey Bug

Lucy Love
123 Heart Road
Valentine, LU 2W5Q6

1002

Pay to Heartland Formal Wear

$190.00

00/100 **dollars**

For: wedding dress

Lucy Love

Write the amount of each check in word form on the line.

Bill B. Ball
2 Hoop Street
Court, BB 5V8P2

1003

Pay to Oakland Oak Trees

$386.00

00/100 **dollars**

For: season pass

Bill B. Ball

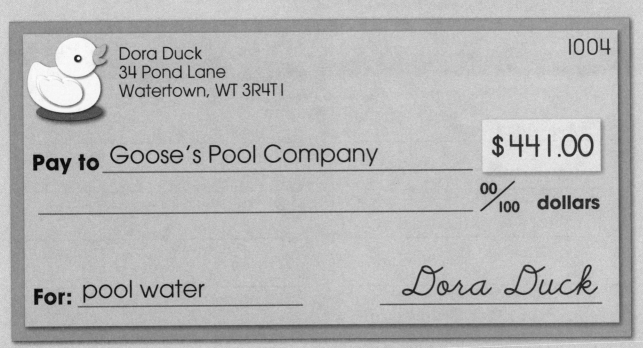

Dora Duck
34 Pond Lane
Watertown, WT 3R4T1

1004

Pay to Goose's Pool Company

$441.00

00/100 **dollars**

For: pool water

Dora Duck

A Day at the Pond

Write two word problems based on the picture. Then, write a number sentence to show how each word problem is solved. Write the correct sign (+ or −) in the box.

_____   _____

_____   _____

_____   _____

_____   _____

____ ☐ ____ = ____   ____ ☐ ____ = ____

Write two word problems based on the picture. Then, write a number sentence to show how each word problem is solved. Write the correct sign (+ or –) in the box.

_____   _____

_____   _____

_____   _____

_____   _____

____ □ ____ = ____   ____ □ ____ = ____

Fractional Flutter

Use counters to show each story. Draw a picture of each story in the box. Then, answer each question.

Four butterflies are on a bush. One is pink. The others are orange.

Three blue birds are eating at the bird feeder. Two red birds are eating at the bird feeder.

What fraction of the butterflies are pink? _____

What fraction of the birds are blue? _____

What fraction of the butterflies are orange? _____

What fraction of the birds are red? _____

Fractional Flutter

Use counters to show each story. Draw a picture of each story in the box. Then, answer each question.

Three butterflies are on a bush. One is yellow. The others are red.

Two blue birds are eating at the bird feeder. Three green birds are eating at the bird feeder.

What fraction of the butterflies are yellow? _____

What fraction of the butterflies are red? _____

What fraction of the birds are blue? _____

What fraction of the birds are green? _____

Thinking Kids™ Math
Grade 2

© Carson-Dellosa
CD-704463

Pizza Pieces

Draw lines to divide the pizzas into equal slices to serve groups of 2, 3, and 4 people. Then, answer the questions.

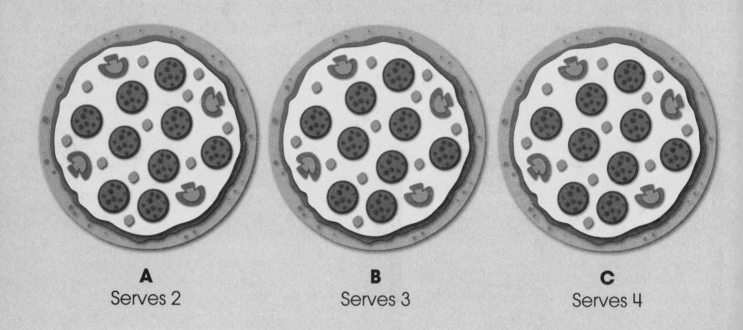

A
Serves 2

B
Serves 3

C
Serves 4

Which pizza shows everyone getting $\frac{1}{3}$ of the pizza? _____

If one person ate $\frac{1}{2}$ of pizza A and two people share the other $\frac{1}{2}$ equally, what fraction of the whole pizza do the two people get? _____

If three people each eat 1 slice of pizza C, what fraction of the pizza is left? _____

Draw lines to divide the pizzas into equal slices to serve groups of 6 and 8 people. Then, answer the questions.

A
Serves 6

B
Serves 8

Which pizza has the largest slices? _____

Which pizza has the smallest slices? _____

What happens to the size of the pizza slices

as you cut the pieces to serve more people? _____

Drop 10 counters onto the hand. Count how many of each color you see. Write the numbers in the number sentences. Repeat until you make 6 different combinations that equal 10.

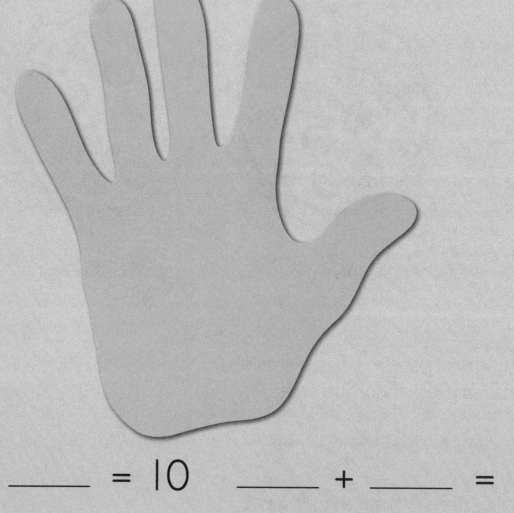

_____ + _____ = 10   _____ + _____ = 10

_____ + _____ = 10   _____ + _____ = 10

_____ + _____ = 10   _____ + _____ = 10

Drop 20 counters onto the hand. Count how many of each color you see. Write the numbers in the number sentences. Repeat until you make 6 different combinations that equal 20.

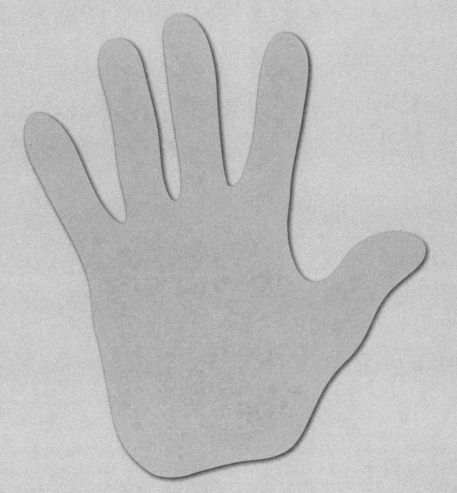

_____ + _____ = 20   _____ + _____ = 20

_____ + _____ = 20   _____ + _____ = 20

_____ + _____ = 20   _____ + _____ = 20

Find the 10s

Circle the two numbers in each row that equal 10. Then, write the third number in the number sentence with 10 and solve for the sum. The first one has been done for you.

$12 + \boxed{9} + \boxed{1} = 10 + \underline{12} = \underline{22}$

$7 + 26 + 3 = 10 + \underline{} = \underline{}$

$2 + 90 + 8 = 10 + \underline{} = \underline{}$

 $5 + 86 + 5 = 10 + \underline{} = \underline{}$

$6 + 4 + 31 = 10 + \underline{} = \underline{}$

Thinking Kids™ Math
Grade 2

© Carson-Dellosa
CD-704463

Circle the two numbers in each row that equal 20. Then, write the third number in the number sentence with 20 and solve for the sum. The first one has been done for you.

 $12 + ⃝18 + ⃝2 = 20 + \underline{12} = \underline{32}$

 $13 + 29 + 7 = 20 + \underline{} = \underline{}$

 $8 + 80 + 12 = 20 + \underline{} = \underline{}$

 $10 + 97 + 10 = 20 + \underline{} = \underline{}$

 $14 + 6 + 41 = 20 + \underline{} = \underline{}$

Addition Breakdown

Add each pair of numbers by breaking the second number into tens and ones. Then, add the groups of ten and add the ones. The first two have been started for you.

56 + 23 =

⬇

56 + 20 + 3 =

⬇

76 + 3 =

⬇

_____

28 + 14 =

⬇

28 + 10 + 4 =

⬇

_____ + _____ =

⬇

_____

46 + 39 =

⬇

_____ + _____ + _____ =

⬇

_____ + _____ =

⬇

_____

32 + 17 =

⬇

_____ + _____ + _____ =

⬇

_____ + _____ =

⬇

_____

Addition Breakdown

Add each pair of numbers by breaking the second number into tens and ones. Then, add the groups of ten and add the ones. The first two have been started for you.

$57 + 33 =$
⬇
$57 + 30 + 3 =$
⬇
$87 + 3 =$
⬇
_____

$25 + 13 =$
⬇
$25 + 10 + 3 =$
⬇
_____ + _____ =
⬇
_____

$48 + 34 =$
⬇
_____ + _____ + _____ =
⬇
_____ + _____ =
⬇
_____

$37 + 18 =$
⬇
_____ + _____ + _____ =
⬇
_____ + _____ =
⬇
_____

Mystery Numbers

Use counters to help you find the missing number behind each magnifying lens. Write a number sentence to solve for the missing number. Then, write the answer.

77 − = 70

_____ _____ = _____

 = _____

29 − = 17

_____ _____ = _____

 = _____

Use counters to help you find the missing number behind each magnifying lens. Write a number sentence to solve for the missing number. Then, write the answer.

21 – ⬡ = 10

_____ ▢ _____ = _____

⬡ = _____

37 – ⬡ = 15

_____ ▢ _____ = _____

⬡ = _____

© Carson-Dellosa
CD-704463

Square Subtraction

Use the hundred board to solve each problem. Circle the first number in the problem on the board. Then, draw a path on the board as you count back to subtract the second number. Draw a triangle around the answer. Write the answer to complete the number sentence.

22 – 11 = _____   67 – 14 = _____   36 – 9 = _____

88 – 12 = _____   94 – 5 = _____   51 – 12 = _____

1	2	3	4	5	6	7	8	9	10
11	12	13	14	15	16	17	18	19	20
21	22	23	24	25	26	27	28	29	30
31	32	33	34	35	36	37	38	39	40
41	42	43	44	45	46	47	48	49	50
51	52	53	54	55	56	57	58	59	60
61	62	63	64	65	66	67	68	69	70
71	72	73	74	75	76	77	78	79	80
81	82	83	84	85	86	87	88	89	90
91	92	93	94	95	96	97	98	99	100

Use the hundred board to solve each problem. Circle the first number in the problem on the board. Then, draw a path on the board as you count back to subtract the second number. Draw a triangle around the answer. Write the answer to complete the number sentence.

31 – 10 = _____   57 – 13 = _____   19 – 8 = _____

77 – 12 = _____   99 – 6 = _____   88 – 10 = _____

1	2	3	4	5	6	7	8	9	10
11	12	13	14	15	16	17	18	19	20
21	22	23	24	25	26	27	28	29	30
31	32	33	34	35	36	37	38	39	40
41	42	43	44	45	46	47	48	49	50
51	52	53	54	55	56	57	58	59	60
61	62	63	64	65	66	67	68	69	70
71	72	73	74	75	76	77	78	79	80
81	82	83	84	85	86	87	88	89	90
91	92	93	94	95	96	97	98	99	100

© Carson-Dellosa
CD-704463

Dip into Dominoes

Count the dots on each side of each domino. Then, write the related facts for each domino.

___ + ___ = ___

___ + ___ = ___

___ − ___ = ___

___ − ___ = ___

___ + ___ = ___

___ + ___ = ___

___ − ___ = ___

___ − ___ = ___

Dip into Dominoes

Count the dots on each side of each domino. Then, write the related facts for each domino.

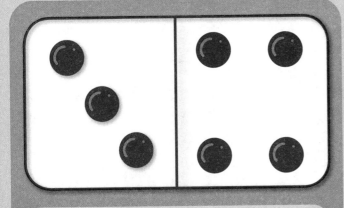

___ + ___ = ___

___ + ___ = ___

___ − ___ = ___

___ − ___ = ___

___ + ___ = ___

___ + ___ = ___

___ − ___ = ___

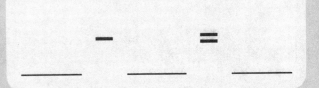

___ − ___ = ___

Thinking Kids™ Math
Grade 2

© Carson-Dellosa
CD-704463

Elevator Operator

Look at the first and last numbers in each number sentence. Did the first number go up or down to become the last number? Circle the correct elevator button beside the number sentence. Write + or – in the blank to make the sentence true.

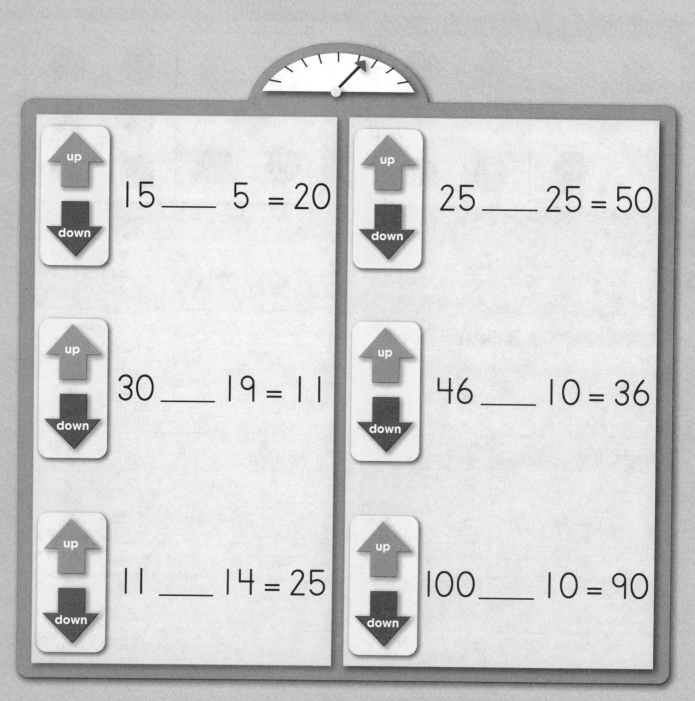

up / down $15 \_\_\_ 5 = 20$

up / down $25 \_\_\_ 25 = 50$

up / down $30 \_\_\_ 19 = 11$

up / down $46 \_\_\_ 10 = 36$

up / down $11 \_\_\_ 14 = 25$

up / down $100 \_\_\_ 10 = 90$

Thinking Kids™ Math
Grade 2

Elevator Operator

Look at the first and last numbers in each number sentence. Did the first number go up or down to become the last number? Circle the correct elevator button beside the number sentence. Write + or – in the blank to make the sentence true.

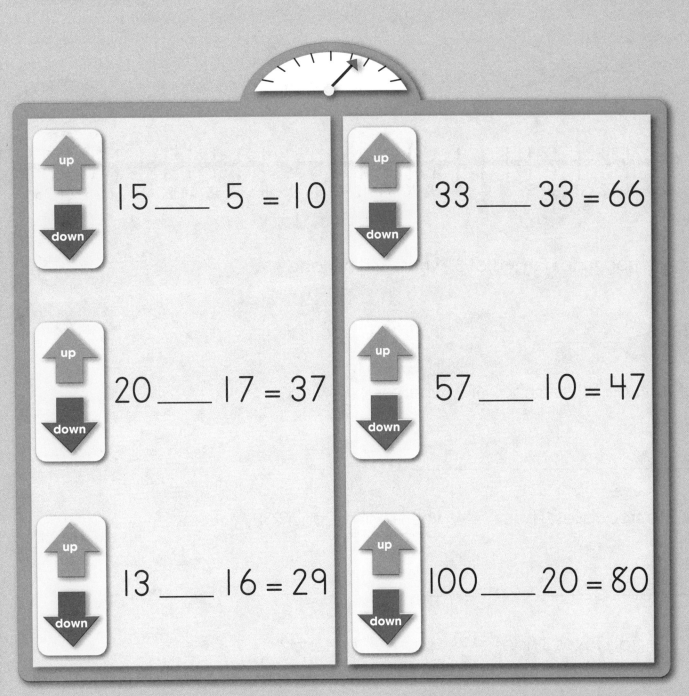

15 ___ $5 = 10$

33 ___ $33 = 66$

20 ___ $17 = 37$

57 ___ $10 = 47$

13 ___ $16 = 29$

100 ___ $20 = 80$

Hopping on a Number Line

Use a counter and the number line to help you write multiplication sentences and answer the questions.

0 1 2 3 4 5 6 7 8 9 10 11 12 13 14 15 16 17 18 19 20 21 22 23 24 25

If the frog takes 5 hops of 3, where will he land?

5 × 3 = _____

If the frog takes 6 hops of 2, where will he land?

_____ × _____ = _____

If the frog takes 4 hops of 4, where will he land?

_____ × _____ = _____

If the frog takes 3 hops of 7, where will he land?

_____ × _____ = _____

Hopping on a Number Line

Use a counter and the number line to help you write multiplication sentences and answer the questions.

0 1 2 3 4 5 6 7 8 9 10 11 12 13 14 15 16 17 18 19 20 21 22 23 24 25

If the frog takes 5 hops of 2, where will he land?

$5 \times 2 =$ _____

If the frog takes 6 hops of 3, where will he land?

_____ $\times$ _____ $=$ _____

If the frog takes 3 hops of 3, where will he land?

_____ $\times$ _____ $=$ _____

If the frog takes 4 hops of 6, where will he land?

_____ $\times$ _____ $=$ _____

© Carson-Dellosa
CD-704463

Fruitful Arrays

Count the fruit in each array. Write two number sentences to describe each array. In the last box, draw your own array and write two number sentences to describe it.

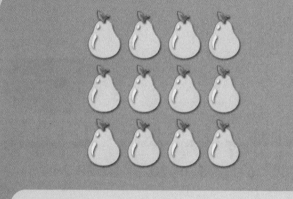

_____ + _____ + _____ = _____

_____ × _____ = _____

_____ + _____ = _____

_____ × _____ = _____

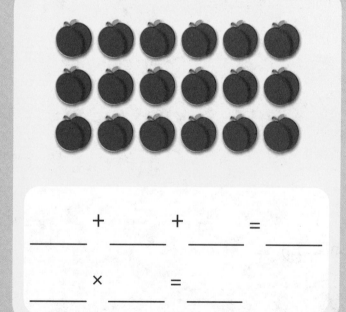

_____ + _____ + _____ = _____

_____ × _____ = _____

Count the fruit in each array. Write two number sentences to describe each array. In the last box, draw your own array and write two number sentences to describe it.

_____ + _____ + _____ = _____

_____ × _____ = _____

_____ + _____ = _____

_____ × _____ = _____

_____ + _____ + _____ = _____

_____ × _____ = _____

© Carson-Dellosa
CD-704463

The Great Divide

Show 4 ways that you can divide 20 counters into equal groups. Draw each way on a planet.

Share and Share Alike

Rachel has treats to share with her 3 dogs. Circle 3 equal groups in each jar. Complete the sentences. Then, write a division number sentence and solve.

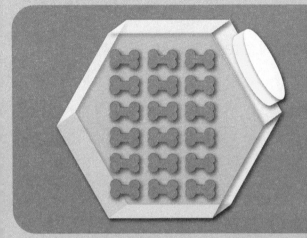

Three dogs shared _____ bones.

Each dog ate _____ bones.

_____ ÷ _____ = _____

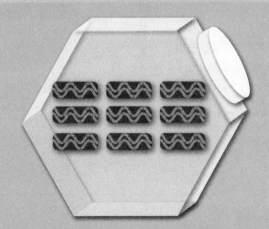

Three dogs shared _____ strips.

Each dog ate _____ strips.

_____ ÷ _____ = _____

Three dogs shared _____ cookies.

Each dog ate _____ cookies.

_____ ÷ _____ = _____

Share and Share Alike

Jim has treats to share with his 4 dogs. Circle 4 equal groups in each jar. Complete the sentences. Then, write a division number sentence and solve.

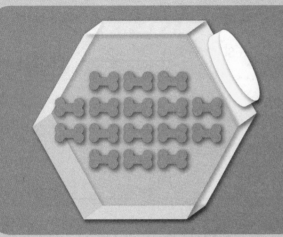

Four dogs shared _____ bones.

Each dog ate _____ bones.

_____ ÷ _____ = _____

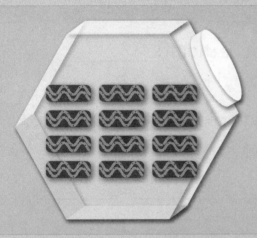

Four dogs shared _____ strips.

Each dog ate _____ strips.

_____ ÷ _____ = _____

Four dogs shared _____ cookies.

Each dog ate _____ cookies.

_____ ÷ _____ = _____

What Should You Do?

Read each word problem. Draw a picture or an array to solve each problem. Write the number sentence.

There are 36 books on 4 shelves. Each shelf has the same number of books on it. How many books are on each shelf?

_____ ☐ _____ = _____books

There are 8 baskets. Each basket has 5 apples in it. How many apples are there in all?

_____ ☐ _____ = _____ apples

Read each word problem. Draw a picture or an array to solve each problem. Write the number sentence.

Logan is paying for himself and 3 friends to go to the movies. The tickets cost $7 each. How much money does he need?

_____ ☐ _____ = $ _____

A clown at a party has 24 balloons. There are 6 children at the party. How many balloons will each child get?

_____ ☐ _____ = _____ balloons

Double Duos

Use doubles addition facts to find each sum.

5 + 5 = _____   3 + 4 = _____   **Think:**
                                      3 + 3 + 1

9 + 9 = _____   6 + 7 = _____   **Think:**
                                      6 + 6 + 1

2 + 2 = _____   4 + 5 = _____   **Think:**
                                      4 + 4 + 1

7 + 7 = _____   8 + 9 = _____   **Think:**
                                      8 + 8 + 1

Double Duos

Use doubles addition facts to find each sum.

4 + 4 = _____   2 + 3 = _____   **Think:** 2 + 2 + 1

8 + 8 = _____   7 + 8 = _____   **Think:** 7 + 7 + 1

3 + 3 = _____   1 + 2 = _____   **Think:** 1 + 1 + 1

6 + 6 = _____   5 + 6 = _____   **Think:** 5 + 5 + 1

Take the Shortcut

Use the shortcuts to find each difference.

– 8 Shortcut	**– 9 Shortcut**
Think: –10, +2	**Think:** –10, +1

14 – 8

_____ – _10_ + _2_ = _____

30 – 9

_____ – _10_ + _1_ = _____

20 – 8

_____ – _10_ + _____ = _____

40 – 9

_____ – _10_ + _____ = _____

Thinking Kids™ Math
Grade 2

55

© Carson-Dellosa
CD-704463

Take the Shortcut

Use the shortcuts to find each difference.

– 8 Shortcut	– 9 Shortcut
Think: –10, +2	**Think:** –10, +1

13 – 8

___ – 10 + 2 = ___

20 – 9

___ – 10 + 1 = ___

30 – 8

___ – 10 + ___ = ___

30 – 9

___ – 10 + ___ = ___

The Estimation Shop

You have $1.00. Estimate to find out if you have enough money to buy the items listed. Use coins to check your answers. Then, circle yes or no.

Do you have enough to buy a yo-yo and a top?

yes   no

Do you have enough to buy a toy train and a toy sailboat?

yes   no

Do you have enough to buy a ball and a teddy bear?

yes   no

Do you have enough to buy a pencil and a toy sailboat?

yes   no

The Estimation Shop

You have $1.25. Estimate to find out if you have enough money to buy the items listed. Use coins to check your answers. Then, circle yes or no.

Do you have enough to buy a toy train and a pencil?

yes   no

Do you have enough to buy a toy train and a yo-yo?

yes   no

Do you have enough to buy a ball and a toy sailboat?

yes   no

Do you have enough to buy a pencil and a yo-yo?

yes   no

Thinking Kids™ Math
Grade 2

© Carson-Dellosa
CD-704463

Brain Power

Use mental math to find each sum. (Hint: Make tens or multiples of 10 first.) Then, write in the cloud how you solved each problem.

12 + 5 + 8 + 5 =

31 + 7 + 3 =

7 + 9 + 13 =

80 + 19 + 1 =

Brain Power

Use mental math to find each sum. (Hint: Make tens or multiples of 10 first.) Then, write in the cloud how you solved each problem.

$13 + 4 + 7 + 4 =$

$41 + 8 + 2 =$

$8 + 7 + 14 =$

$70 + 18 + 3 =$

Thinking Kids™ Math
Grade 2

© Carson-Dellosa
CD-704463

The Speed Machine

Use a calculator to solve each problem.

$84 + 56 =$ _____

$93 - 47 =$ _____

$36 + 19 + 55 =$ _____

$703 - 284 =$ _____

$563 + 459 =$ _____

$1{,}001 - 699 =$ _____

The Speed Machine

Use a calculator to solve each problem.

85 + 66 = _____

92 – 44 = _____

34 + 18 + 56 = _____

707 – 167 = _____

571 + 455 = _____

1,010 – 688 = _____

Clothing Sort

Sort and classify the clothing into groups. Then, on a separate sheet of paper, write how you classified each group.

© Carson-Dellosa
CD-704463

Breaking the Rules

Look at the shapes in each row. Name the sorting rule for each group. Follow the directions to show 3 shape blocks that do not fit the rule. Then, draw the shapes.

Rule: _____   Show 3 blocks that would break the rule.

Rule: _____   Show 3 blocks that would break the rule.

Rule: _____   Show 3 blocks that would break the rule.

Thinking Kids™ Math
Grade 2

© Carson-Dellosa
CD-704463

Bead a Pattern

Put counters on the blank beads to continue each pattern.

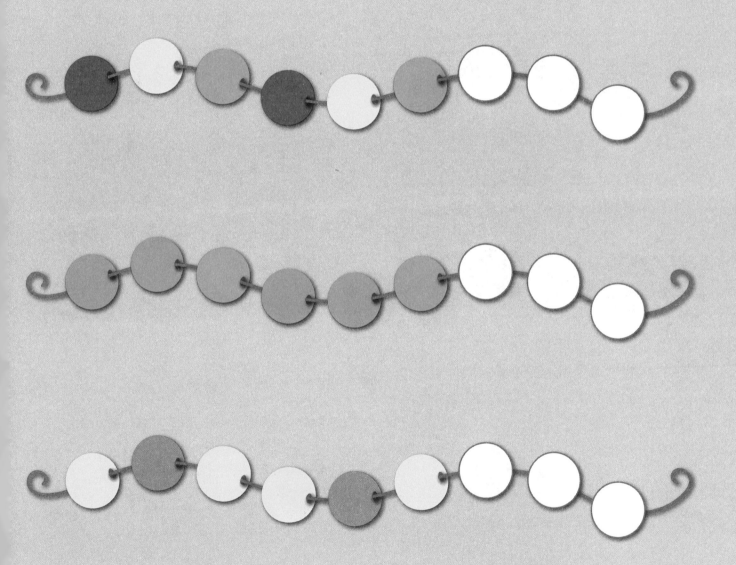

© Carson-Dellosa
CD-704463

Bead a Pattern

Put counters on the blank beads to continue each pattern.

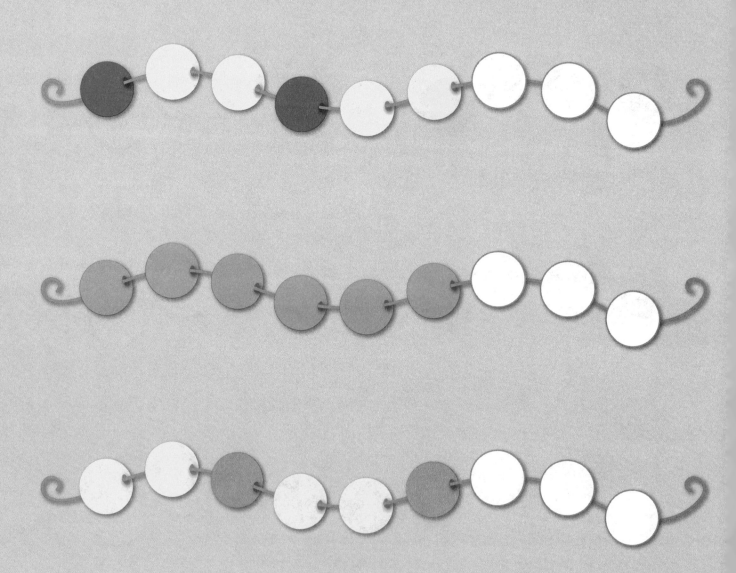

Buzzing Around

Write the missing numbers in each row of flowers.

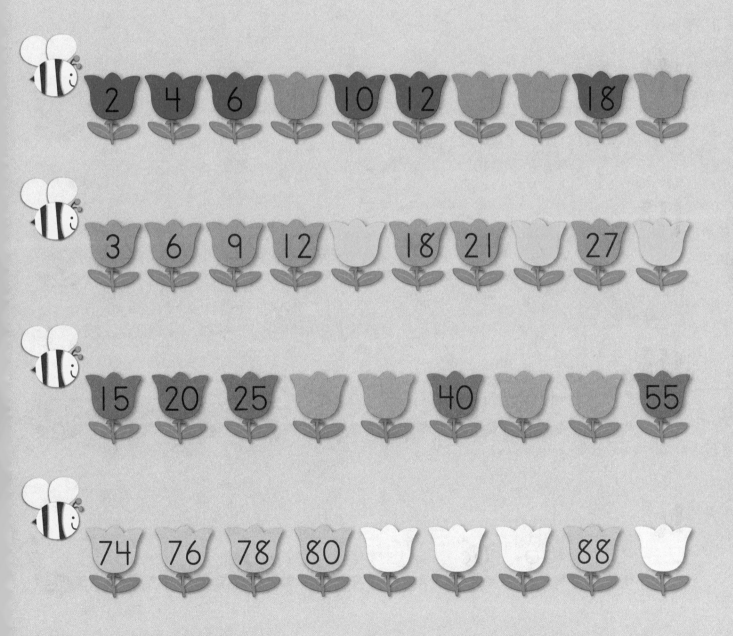

Row 1: 2, 4, 6, ___, 10, 12, ___, ___, 18, ___

Row 2: 3, 6, 9, 12, ___, 18, 21, ___, 27, ___

Row 3: 15, 20, 25, ___, ___, 40, ___, ___, 55

Row 4: 74, 76, 78, 80, ___, ___, ___, 88, ___

Thinking Kids™ Math
Grade 2

© Carson-Dellosa
CD-704463

Buzzing Around

Write the missing numbers in each row of flowers.

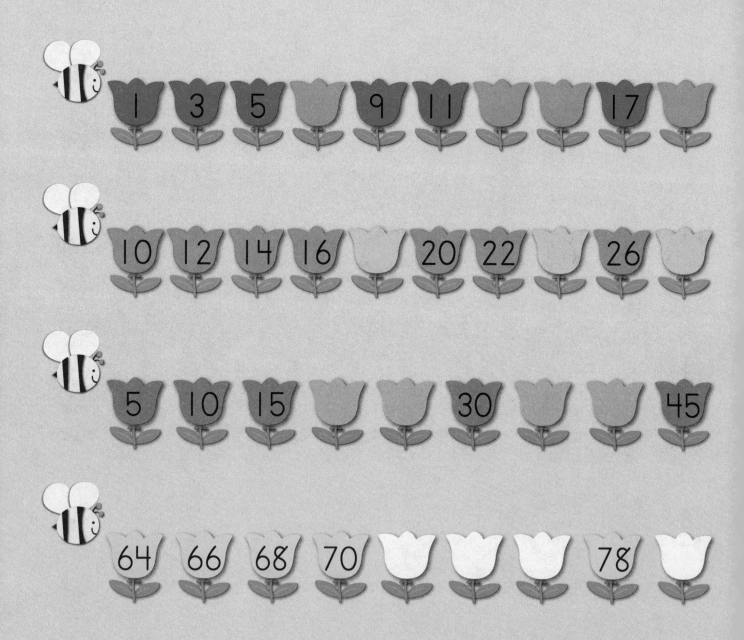

Row 1: 1, 3, 5, ___, 9, 11, ___, ___, 17, ___

Row 2: 10, 12, 14, 16, ___, 20, 22, ___, 26, ___

Row 3: 5, 10, 15, ___, ___, 30, ___, ___, 45

Row 4: 64, 66, 68, 70, ___, ___, ___, 78, ___

Thinking Kids™ Math
Grade 2

© Carson-Dellosa
CD-704463

Draw the shape that comes next in each pattern. Tell whether the shape was slid, turned, or flipped.

Out of This World Patterns

Look at the rules and number patterns. Write the missing rules and numbers.

Rule: +7 ⭐ 14 ⭐ ⭐ ⭐ ⭐ ⭐ ⭐

Rule:___ 19 17 15 13 11 ⭐ 7 ⭐

Rule: −3 ⭐ ⭐ 22 ⭐ ⭐ ⭐ ⭐ ⭐

Rule:___ 85 80 75 ⭐ ⭐ 60 55 ⭐

Put a counter on each circle. Trace each circle. Look at the rules and number patterns. Write the missing rules and numbers.

Rule: +6 — 14

Rule: ___ — 63, 59, 44, 31, 20, __, 12

Rule: −5 — __, __, 65

Rule: ___ — 44, 47, 50, __, __, 59, 62

© Carson-Dellosa
CD-704463

Name That Pattern!

Name each pattern using letters.

____ ____ ____ ____ ____ ____

____ ____ ____ ____ ____ ____

____ ____ ____ ____ ____ ____ ____ ____

Name each pattern using letters.

____ ____ ____ ____ ____ ____

____ ____ ____ ____ ____ ____

____ ____ ____ ____ ____ ____ ____ ____ ____

Puppy Patterns

Name each pattern using letters. Then, use counters to copy the pattern.

Pattern Performances

Clap, snap, or tap each pattern.

What Repeats?

Name each pattern using letters. Circle the repeating parts in each letter pattern. Then, create a matching pattern with counters.

____ ____ ____ ____ ____ ____ ____ ____ ____

____ ____ ____ ____ ____ ____ ____ ____

Name each pattern using letters. Circle the repeating parts in each letter pattern. Then, create a matching pattern with counters.

_____ _____ _____ _____ _____ _____ _____ _____ _____

_____ _____ _____ _____ _____ _____ _____ _____ _____

Bucket of Buttons

Each child named the button pattern in a different way. Explain each child's rule.

A B C A B C A B C

Explain Jayla's rule: _____

A B A A B A A B A

Explain Carson's rule: _____

A A B A A B A A B

Explain Nina's rule: _____

What's the Rule?

Draw what comes next in each pattern.

Thinking Kids™ Math
Grade 2

© Carson-Dellosa
CD-704463

Growing Shapes

Use counters to find out how many squares are needed to make the next 2 sets in each pattern. Then, draw the squares in the boxes.

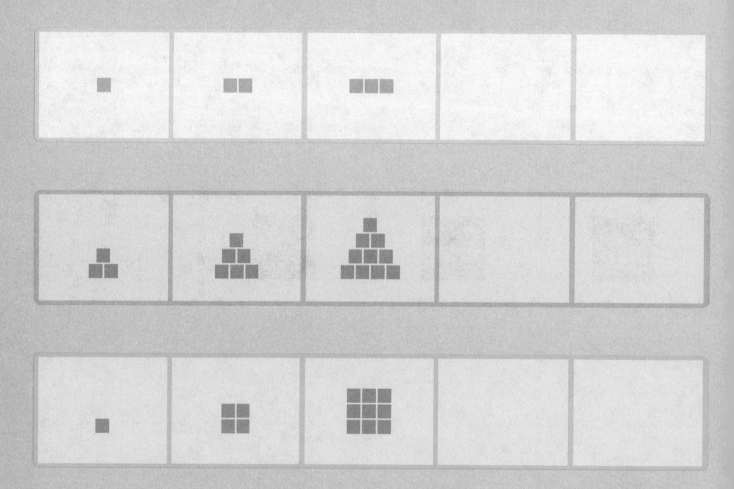

Missing Pieces

Use counters to copy the sets of dots in each pattern and figure out the missing sets. Then, draw each missing set.

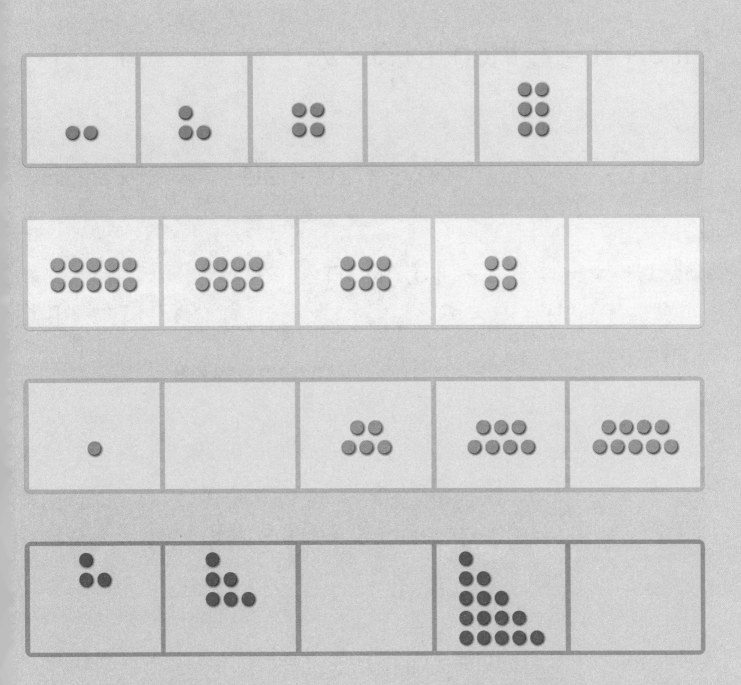

Thinking Kids™ Math
Grade 2

© Carson-Dellosa
CD-704463

True or False?

Use counters to test each number sentence. Then, decide if each statement is true or false. Circle T for true or F for false.

If 3 + 4 = 7, then 4 + 3 = 7.   T   F

If 20 + 0 = 20, then 0 + 20 = 20.   T   F

If 3 + 4 + 4 + 2 = 13, then
13 = 2 + 4 + 4 + 3.   T   F

If 12 − 0 = 12, then 0 − 12 = 12.   T   F

If 23 + 50 = 73, then 73 = 50 + 23.   T   F

If 18 − 9 = 9, then 9 = 9 − 18.   T   F

True or False?

Use counters to test each number sentence. Then, decide if each statement is true or false. Circle T for true or F for false.

If 3 + 5 = 8, then 5 + 3 = 8.   T   F

If 30 + 0 = 30, then 0 + 30 = 30.   T   F

If 2 + 3 + 3 + 5 = 13, then
13 = 5 + 3 + 3 + 2.   T   F

If 13 − 0 = 13, then 0 − 13 = 13.   T   F

If 33 + 60 = 93, then 93 = 60 + 33.   T   F

If 17 − 8 = 9, then 9 = 8 − 17.   T   F

Thinking Kids™ Math
Grade 2

© Carson-Dellosa
CD-704463

Symbol Substitute

Use base ten blocks to figure out the missing number behind each picture. Then, write the number.

$40 +$ ⬤ $= 50$

⬤ $= \underline{\hspace{2cm}}$

🍃 $- 70 = 20$

🍃 $= \underline{\hspace{2cm}}$

$10 +$ ⭐ $= 30$

⭐ $= \underline{\hspace{2cm}}$

$80 -$ 🎈 $= 20$

🎈 $= \underline{\hspace{2cm}}$

Symbol Substitute

Use base ten blocks to figure out the missing number behind each picture. Then, write the number.

$30 + $ ⬤ $= 70$

⬤ $= $ _____

$$\text{🍃} - 60 = 30$$

🍃 $= $ _____

$20 + $ ⭐ $= 40$

⭐ $= $ _____

$90 - $ 🎈 $= 60$

🎈 $= $ _____

Thinking Kids™ Math
Grade 2

© Carson-Dellosa
CD-704463

Greater Than, Less Than

Write >, <, or = in each circle to make each statement true.

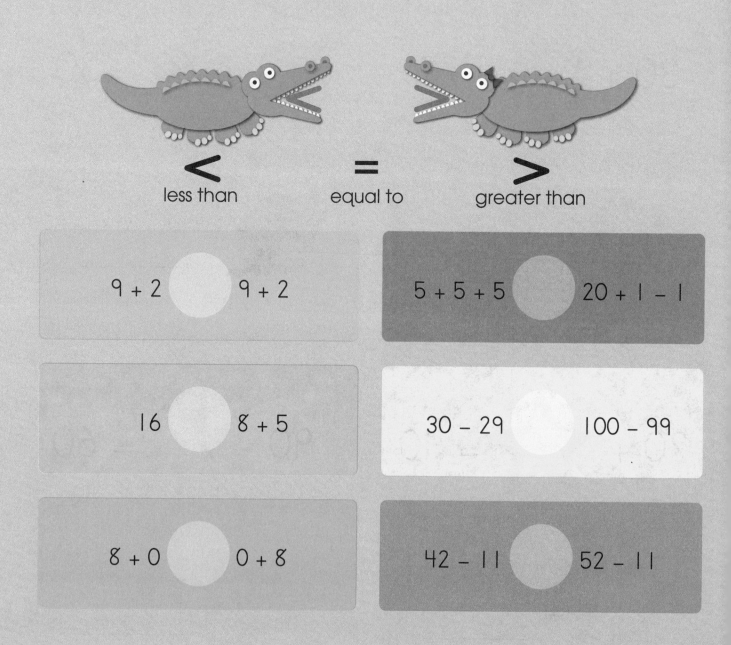

<
less than

=
equal to

>
greater than

9 + 2 ◯ 9 + 2

5 + 5 + 5 ◯ 20 + 1 − 1

16 ◯ 8 + 5

30 − 29 ◯ 100 − 99

8 + 0 ◯ 0 + 8

42 − 11 ◯ 52 − 11

Greater Than, Less Than

Write >, <, or = in each circle to make each statement true.

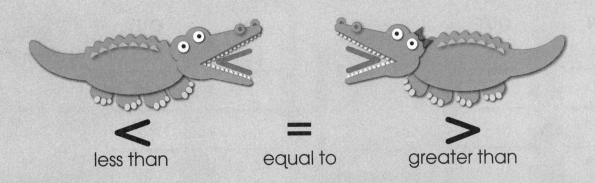

< less than   = equal to   > greater than

8 + 1 ◯ 10 + 11

6 + 6 + 6 ◯ 20 – 1 – 1

17 ◯ 8 + 9

60 – 59 ◯ 99 – 98

9 + 0 ◯ 0 + 9

33 – 11 ◯ 44 – 11

Thinking Kids™ Math
Grade 2

© Carson-Dellosa
CD-704463

Write the missing numbers and rules for each machine.

Machine 1

IN	OUT
8	18
24	34
	43
17	
61	

RULE: _____

Machine 2

IN	OUT
100	95
	49
17	12
99	
	0

RULE: _____

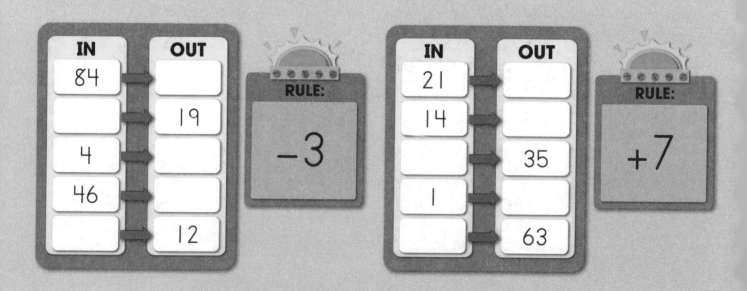

Machine 3

IN	OUT
84	
	19
4	
46	
	12

RULE: −3

Machine 4

IN	OUT
21	
14	
	35
1	
	63

RULE: +7

Mystery Machines

Write the missing numbers and rules for each machine.

Machine 1

IN	OUT
9	17
22	30
	33
16	
69	

RULE: _____

Machine 2

IN	OUT
100	94
	27
41	35
67	
	0

RULE: _____

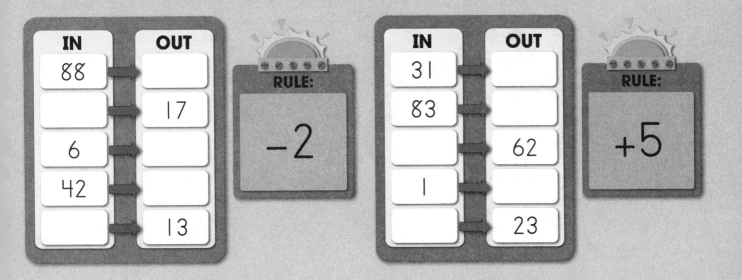

Machine 3

IN	OUT
88	
	17
6	
42	
	13

RULE: −2

Machine 4

IN	OUT
31	
83	
	62
1	
	23

RULE: +5

Count Up and Back

Follow the rules in each box. Write the missing number on each object.

Rules: = + 4   = − 2

12

Rules:  = + 10   = − 20

100

Rules: = + 3   = − 1

18

Follow the rules in each box. Write the missing number on each object.

Rules: = + 5   = – 1

12

Rules: = + 11   = – 22

100

Rules: 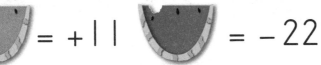 = + 6   = – 4

18

© Carson-Dellosa
CD-704463

What's the Weather?

Read the temperatures on Monday's weather map. Then, read the temperatures on Tuesday's weather map. Write the temperatures for each city. Then, record the difference in temperature for each city.

Monday

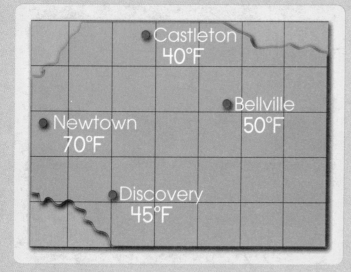

Tuesday

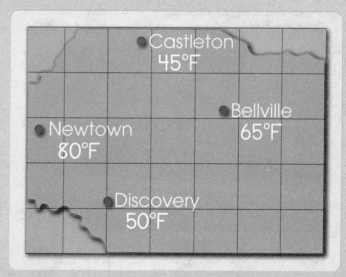

	Monday	Tuesday	Difference
Castleton	_____ °F	_____ °F	_____ °F
Newtown	_____ °F	_____ °F	_____ °F
Bellville	_____ °F	_____ °F	_____ °F
Discovery	_____ °F	_____ °F	_____ °F

Thinking Kids™ Math
Grade 2

© Carson-Dellosa
CD-704463

What's the Weather?

Read the temperatures on Friday's weather map. Then, read the temperatures on Saturday's weather map. Write the temperatures for each city. Then, record the difference in temperature for each city.

Friday

Saturday

	Friday	Saturday	Difference
Castleton	_____ °F	_____ °F	_____ °F
Newtown	_____ °F	_____ °F	_____ °F
Bellville	_____ °F	_____ °F	_____ °F
Discovery	_____ °F	_____ °F	_____ °F

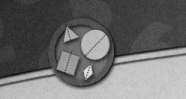

Create a Shape

Use the pattern block of each shape to draw two larger figures. One example has been done for you.

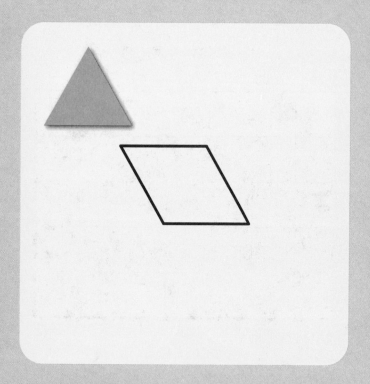

Create a Shape

Use the pattern block of each shape to draw two larger figures. One example has been done for you.

Shape Sorter

Look at each set of shapes. What attributes are the shapes sorted by? Use shape blocks to create a new sort. Write the attributes for the new sort and draw the shapes.

Attributes:

_____

_____

_____

_____

_____

Attributes:

_____

_____

_____

_____

_____

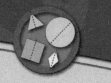

Solve each riddle. Draw and write the name of the two- or three-dimensional figure described. Write your own riddle for the last figure.

I have straight lines. I have four sides that are all equal in length. I have four right angles. What figure am I?

_____

My faces are circles. I can roll and stack. What figure am I?

_____

_____

_____

_____

_____

square pyramid

Name That Figure!

Circle the word that describes each object.

cube

cylinder

sphere

cone

cylinder

sphere

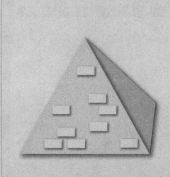
cone

sphere

pyramid

cube

cone

sphere

sphere

cone

rectangular prism

cube

cone

pyramid

Follow the directions.

1. Color each circle.

2. Outline each shape that has 4 sides.

3. Circle each small shape.

4. Draw an X on each square.

5. Draw a dot in each shape with 3 sides.

Angles, Faces, and Sides

Read each description. Circle the correct figure. You may circle more than one figure in each row.

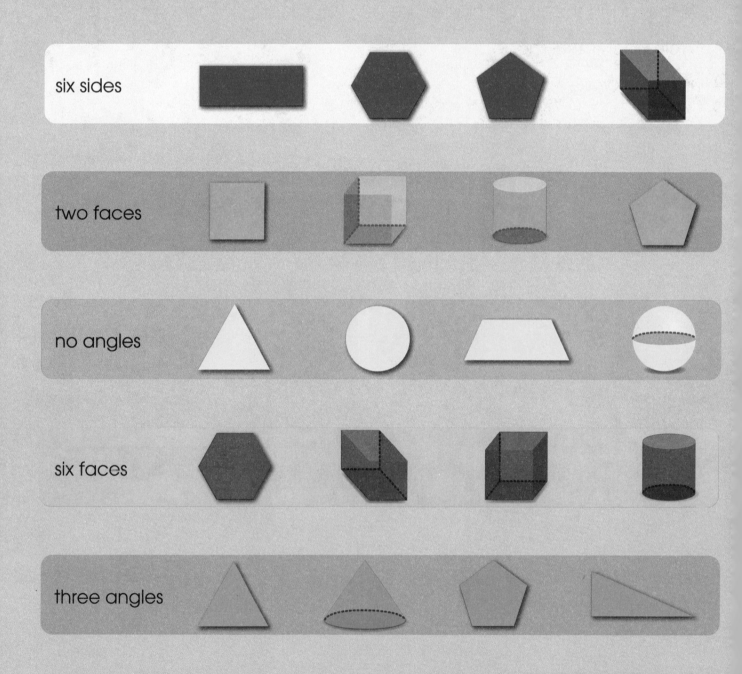

six sides

two faces

no angles

six faces

three angles

Look at each figure. Decide if it will roll, stack, or do both. Circle the answer(s).

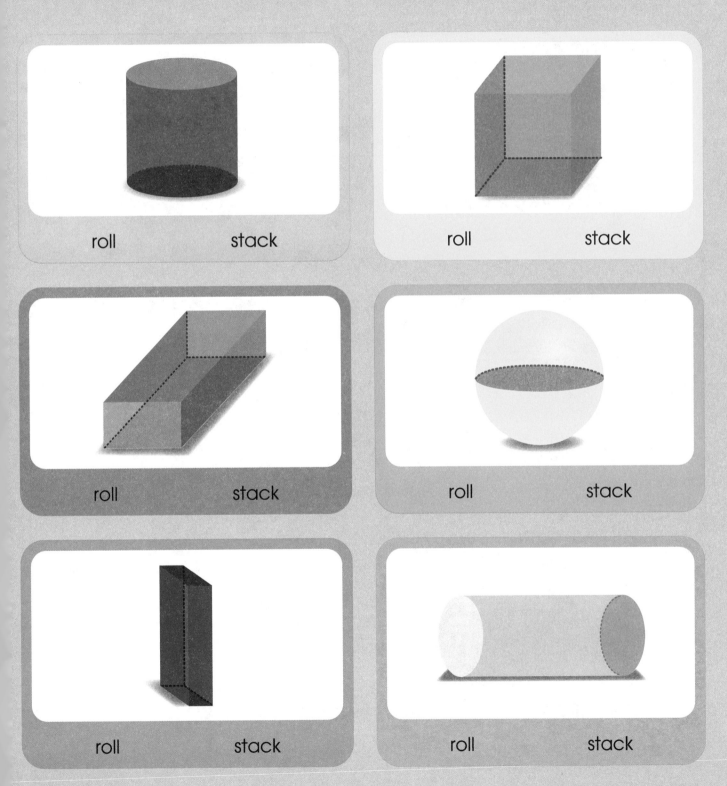

roll   stack

roll   stack

roll   stack

roll   stack

roll   stack

roll   stack

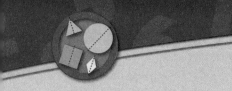

Tangrams

A tangram is a puzzle that has 7 pieces, or tans. Match the tans to the shapes in the yellow square. Then, rearrange the tans in the blue box and trace them to make a new picture.

What can you make?

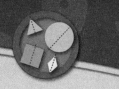

A tangram is a puzzle that has 7 pieces, or tans.

Are any of the shapes congruent?
Similar?
What other shape can you make by putting together the 2 small triangles?

© Carson-Dellosa
CD-704463

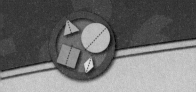

Create a Picture

Draw a picture using 2 hexagons, 6 triangles, 1 trapezoid, 3 squares, and 2 rhombuses.

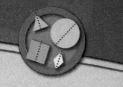
Look at the picture you drew on the previous page. Where is the trapezoid? What word(s) describe the trapezoid's position? Describe the picture you drew using position words such as above, beside, etc.

Penguin Path

Help the penguin get to the fish. On a separate sheet of paper, write the number of steps the penguin needs to take and the directions she needs to travel (north, south, east, or west).

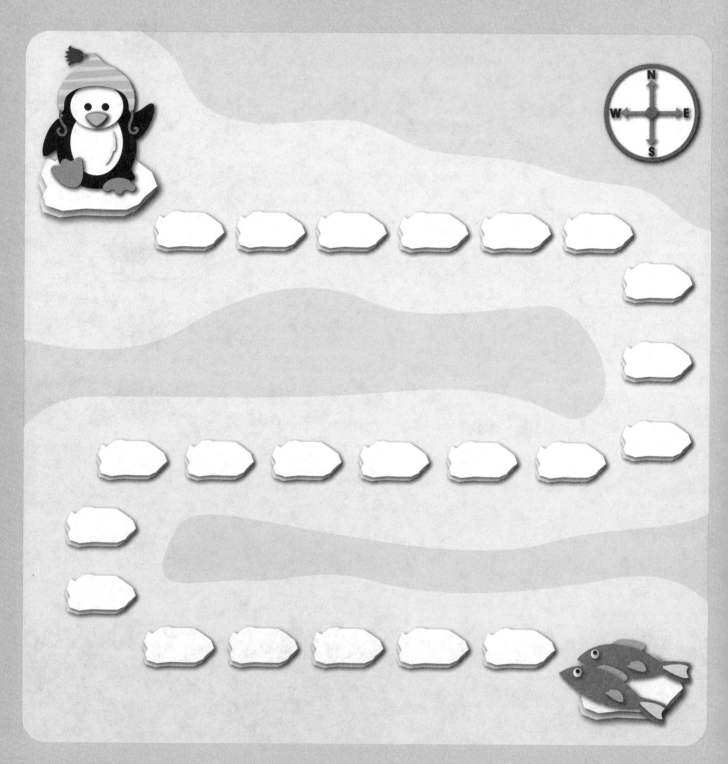

Use your work from the previous page to answer the questions. How many steps did the penguin take in all? Did the penguin take more steps north or more steps south? If another penguin followed your directions, would it end up in the same place as this penguin?

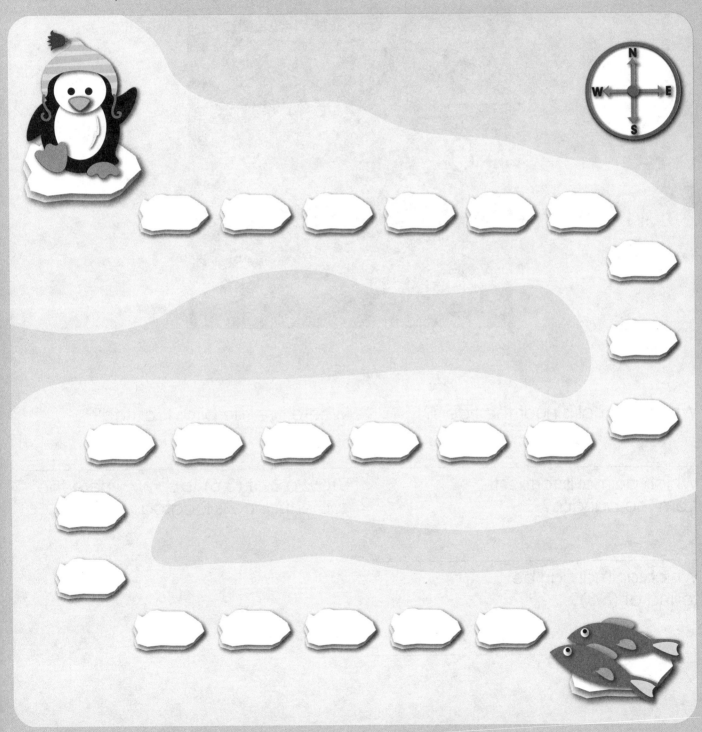

© Carson-Dellosa
CD-704463

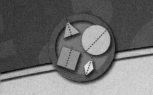

At the Zoo

Use the zoo map to answer each question.

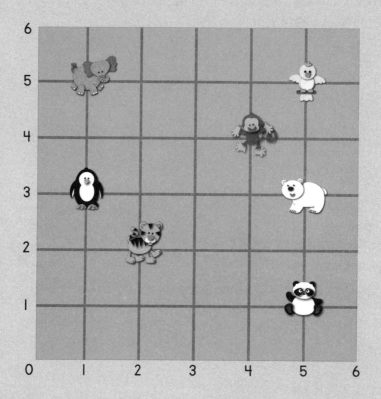

Which animal is near the tigers?

_____

Which animal is farthest
from the pandas?

_____

Which animal can be
found at (5,3)?

_____

Where are the birds located?

_____

Draw a **Z** at (3,6) to show where the
zoo entrance is located.

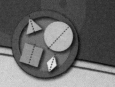

Use the zoo map to answer each question.

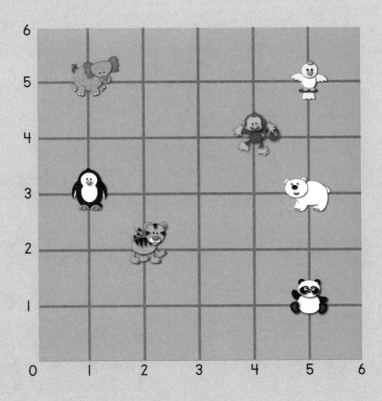

At what coordinates are the monkeys located?

_____

At what coordinates are the pandas located?

_____

Are the tigers and the birds near or far from each other? How do you know?

_____

How many squares down from the birds must you go to get to the polar bears?

_____

© Carson-Dellosa
CD-704463

Draw how each letter would look after a slide, a flip, and a turn.

H	slide	flip	turn
P	slide	flip	turn
S	slide	flip	turn
T	slide	flip	turn

Congruent or Similar?

Look at each set of shapes. Write congruent, similar, or neither. Draw examples of congruent and similar shapes in the boxes.

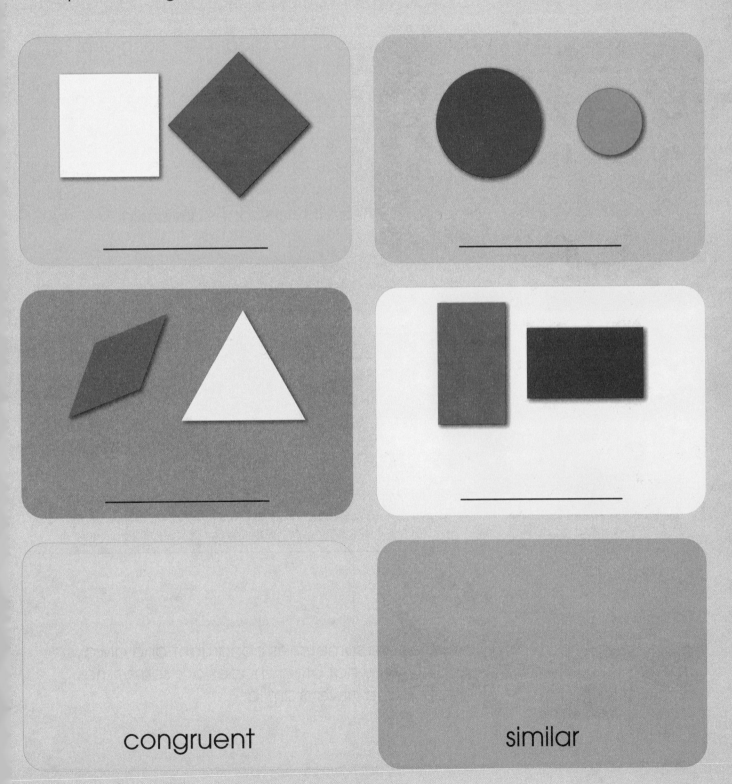

congruent

similar

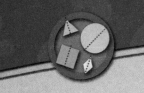

Congruent or Similar?

Look at the shapes and then answer the questions.

What does it mean if two shapes are congruent?

_____

What does it mean if two shapes are similar?

_____

_____

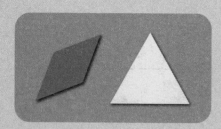

How can two shapes be neither similar nor congruent?

_____

Two circles are sometimes congruent and always similar. Two of what other shapes are sometimes congruent and always similar?

_____

Alphabet Symmetry

Circle each letter of the alphabet that has symmetry. Draw Xs on the letters that do not have symmetry.

A B C D E F

G H I J K L

M N O P Q R

S T U V W X

Y Z

Alphabet Symmetry

Look at the letters of the alphabet and answer the questions.

How many uppercase letters of the alphabet are symmetrical?

_____

Can a shape have more than one line of symmetry?

_____

What shape has the most lines of symmetry?

_____

Which uppercase letters are not symmetrical?

_____

Complete the chart by drawing the correct face for each three-dimensional figure. Then, write the name of each shape that is a face.

figure		
	cylinder	cube
face		

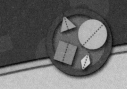

A Bird's Eye View

Complete the chart by drawing the correct face for each three-dimensional figure. Then, write the name of each shape that is a face.

figure		
	pyramid	cone
face		

Look at each outlined shape. Use the length of each side to write a number sentence. Then, use the number sentence to find the perimeter.

_____ + _____ + _____ + _____ + _____ = _____

P = _____

_____ + _____ + _____ + _____ = _____

P = _____

© Carson-Dellosa
CD-704463

Find the Perimeter

Look at each outlined shape. Use the length of each side to write a number sentence. Then, use the number sentence to find the perimeter.

_____ + _____ + _____ + _____ = _____

P = _____

_____ + _____ + _____ = _____

P = _____

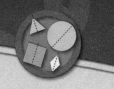

Look around the room for objects that have shapes like those in the picture below. Find at least two objects that are each type of shape. Circle the shapes below when you find them.

Time Will Tell

Circle the unit of time you would use to measure each activity. Then, write the order of the units of time from 1 to 6, with 1 being the shortest unit of time.

brush your teeth

minutes   hours

_____

take a vacation

minutes   days

_____

build a house

hours   months

_____

grow a tree

years   days

_____

tie your shoes

seconds   minutes

_____

bake a cake

hours   week

_____

Time and Time Again

Read the times. Draw the hands and write the numbers for each time given.

five o'clock

three thirty

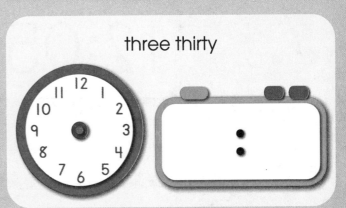

quarter after one

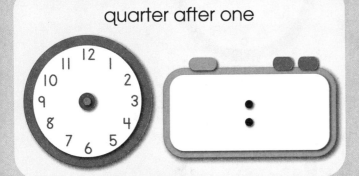

quarter to six

seven o'clock

five minutes after two

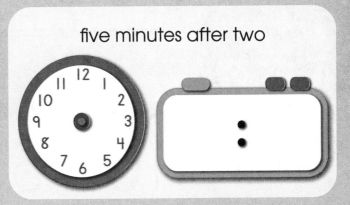

The Hands of Time

Draw the hands to show the time. Repeat for each clock.

The Hands of Time

Write the numbers to show the time. Repeat for each clock.

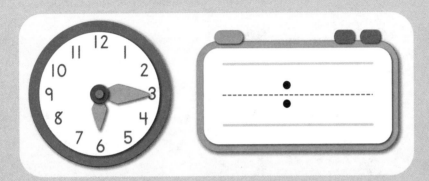

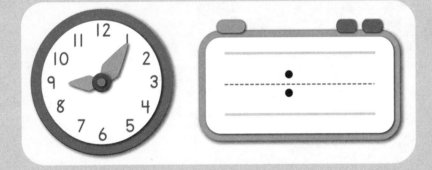

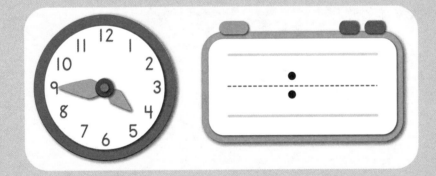

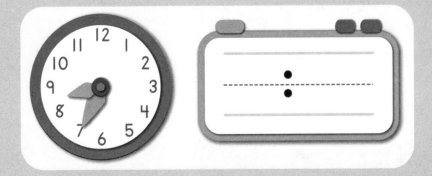

© Carson-Dellosa
CD-704463

The Hands of Time

Draw the hands to show the time. Repeat for each clock.

Write the numbers to show the time. Repeat for each clock.

Time and Time Again

Read the times. Draw the hands and write the numbers for each time given.

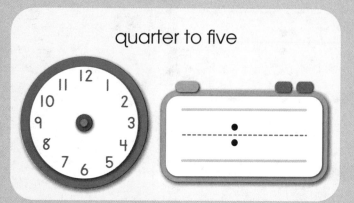

quarter to five

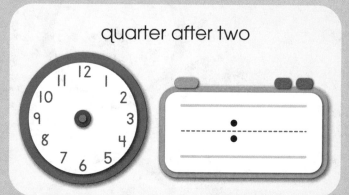

quarter after two

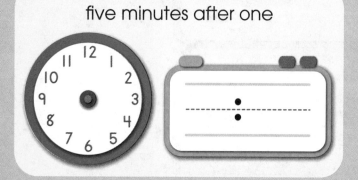

five minutes after one

eight o'clock

four thirty

nine thirty

What Time Is It?

Look at each clock. Write the time.

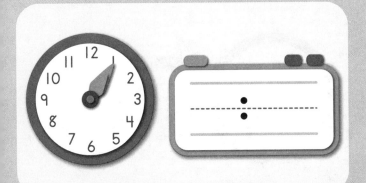

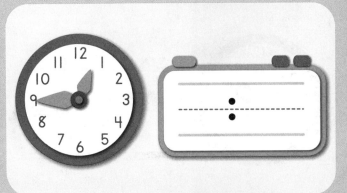

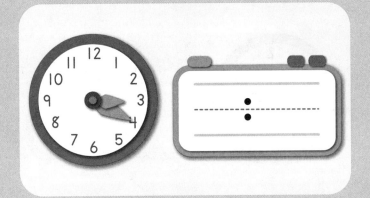

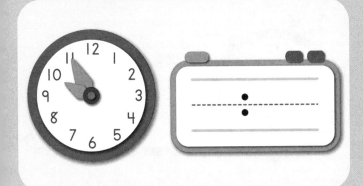

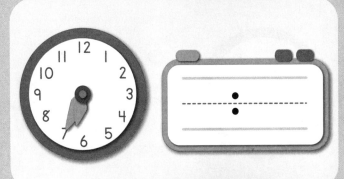

What Time Is It?

Look at each clock. Write the time.

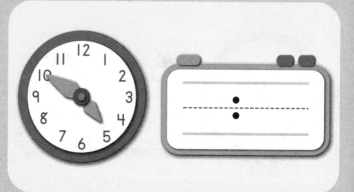

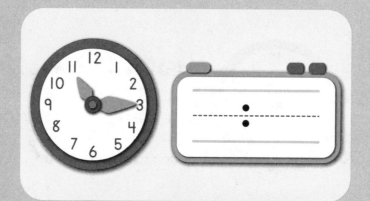

Match the time on the clock with the digital time.

Time Match

Match the time on the clock with the digital time.

6:20

7:30

1:40

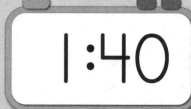
4:15

11:05

Read each word problem. Draw the hands on the first clock to show the start time for the swimmer's laps. Draw the hands on the last clock to show the end time for the laps.

Start

Katie arrived at swim practice at 3:30. She swam her warm-up laps in 30 minutes. What time did she finish?

End

Start

Brady arrived at swim practice at 4:00. He finished his warm-up laps in 45 minutes. What time did he finish?

End

Start

Ethan arrived at swim practice at 3:45. He finished his warm-up laps in 20 minutes. What time did he finish?

End

Elapsed Laps

Read each word problem. Draw the hands on the first clock to show the start time for the swimmer's laps. Draw the hands on the last clock to show the end time for the laps.

Start

Lisa arrived at swim practice at 2:30. She swam her warm-up laps in 30 minutes. What time did she finish?

End

Start

Tom arrived at swim practice at 3:00. He finished his warm-up laps in 35 minutes. What time did he finish?

End

Start

Jake arrived at swim practice at 2:45. He finished his warm-up laps in 40 minutes. What time did he finish?

End

Write the names of two objects or draw two objects on each scale to make the picture true.

A Balancing Act

Write the names of two objects or draw two objects on each scale to make the picture true.

Biggest Blankets

Use counters to find the area (A) of each blanket.

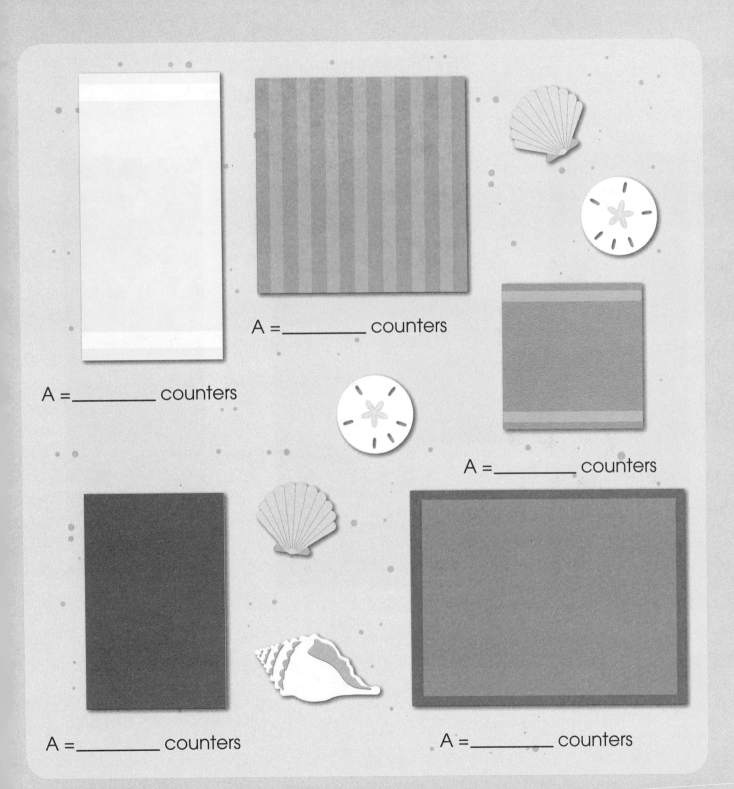

A =_____ counters

A =_____ counters

A =_____ counters

A =_____ counters

A =_____ counters

What's Inside?

Use counters to find the area (A) of each letter.

A = _____ counters   A = _____ counters

© Carson-Dellosa
CD-704463

Measure the length of each object with counters. Write the measurement on the line.

_____ counters

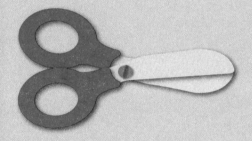

_____ counters

_____ counters

Cube Counts

Measure the length of each object with counters. Write the measurement on the line.

_____ counters

_____ counters

_____ counters

eraser

Measure the length of each bug with paper clips. Write the measurement on the line.

The ladybug is about _____ paper clip(s) long.

The bee is about _____ paper clip(s) long.

Measure the length of the butterfly with paper clips. Write the measurement on the line.

The butterfly is about _____ paper clips long.

Measure Up!

Estimate the length of a desk or a table. Then, measure it with each item.

Estimate: _____ paper clips long

Actual: _____ paper clips long

Estimate: _____ pencils long

Actual: _____ pencils long

Estimate: _____ paintbrushes long

Actual: _____ paintbrushes long

Estimate: _____ scissors long

Actual: _____ scissors long

Thinking Kids™ Math
Grade 2

© Carson-Dellosa
CD-704463

Ribbon Measurement

Use the width of your thumb to measure the length of each ribbon.

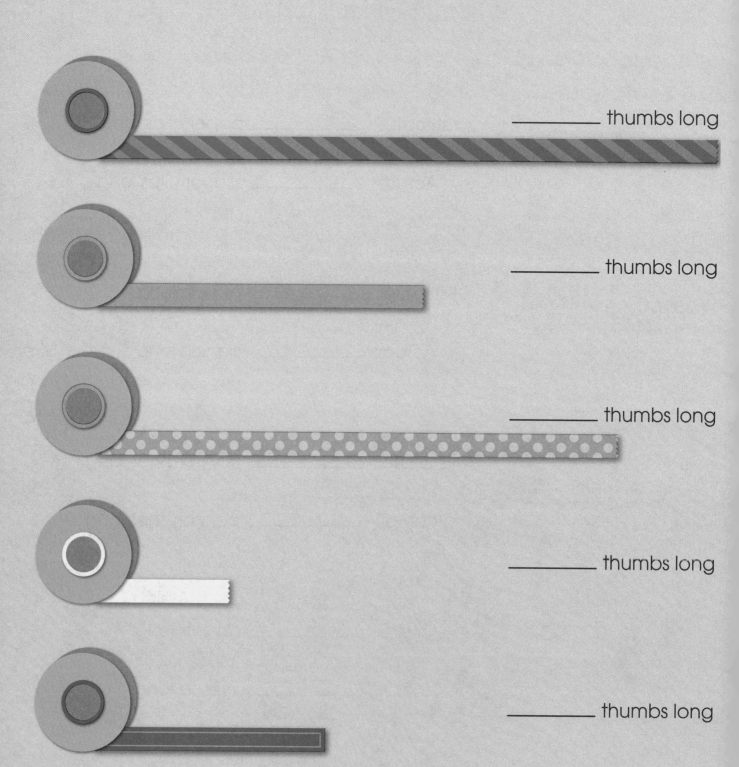

_____ thumbs long

_____ thumbs long

_____ thumbs long

_____ thumbs long

_____ thumbs long

Thinking Kids™ Math
Grade 2

Measure each dog with a ruler.

The pug is _____ inch long.

The beagle is _____ inches long.

Darling Dogs

Measure each dog with a ruler.

The poodle is _____ inches long.

The dachshund is _____ inches long.

Collecting Data

Sort a set of counters by color. Complete the tally chart to show your data. Then, answer the questions.

Color	Number

How many total counters are there? _____

Which color appears the most? _____

Which color appears the least? _____

© Carson-Dellosa
CD-704463

Where Does It Go?

Look at the shirts. How would you sort and classify them into groups? Label each side of the Venn diagram with an attribute. Then, write each shirt number in the correct section.

_____   both   _____

One for the Money

Sort a handful of coins. Arrange the pennies, nickels, dimes, and quarters on the graph to show how many of each coin you have.

Totals: _____ pennies, _____ nickels, _____ dimes, _____ quarters

Thinking Kids™ Math
Grade 2

Count the coins and write the amount.

5¢   1¢
   5¢

_____ ¢

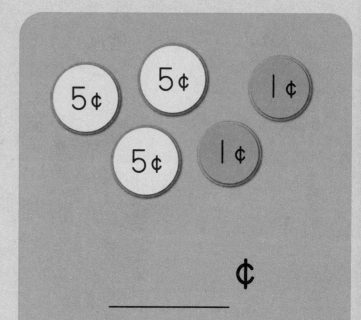

5¢   5¢   1¢
   5¢   1¢

_____ ¢

5¢
1¢
1¢

_____ ¢

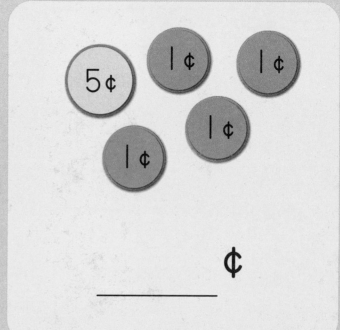

5¢   1¢   1¢
   1¢
1¢

_____ ¢

Pennies, Nickles, and Dimes

Count the coins and write the amount.

_____ ¢

_____ ¢

_____ ¢

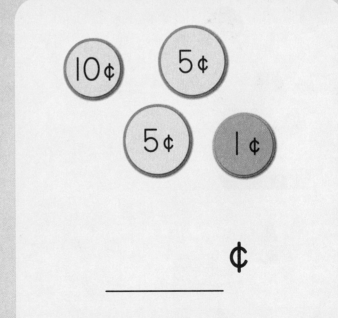

_____ ¢

Draw a line from the toy to the amount of money it costs.

36¢

68¢

43¢

57¢

22¢

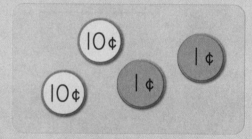

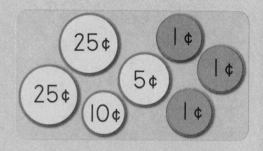

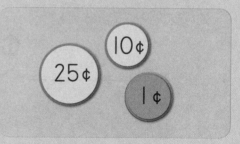

Count the money and write the amounts.

10¢ 10¢ 10¢ 10¢ 10¢
10¢ 10¢ 10¢ 10¢ 10¢

$ ____ . ____

25¢ 25¢
25¢ 25¢

$ ____ . ____

$1   25¢

$ ____ . ____

$1
10¢ 10¢ 1¢

$ ____ . ____

$1   25¢ 25¢   5¢

$ ____ . ____

25¢ 25¢ 10¢ 10¢ 1¢
25¢ 25¢ 5¢ 1¢

$ ____ . ____

Lunch Time

Draw a line from each food item to the correct amount of money.

$ 1.59

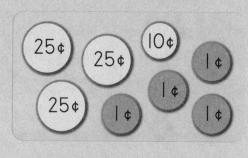

$ .77

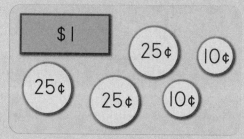

$ 1.95

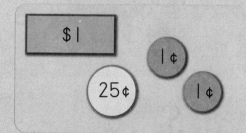

$ 1.27

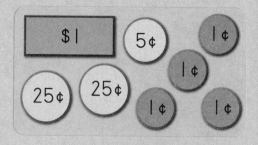

$ .89

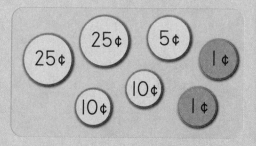

Thinking Kids™ Math
Grade 2

Look at the results of a class survey about favorite pets. Draw smiley faces to show the data in a pictograph. Look at the key to see how many votes each smiley face stands for.

Ⅲ Ⅱ Ⅰ	Ⅲ Ⅱ Ⅲ Ⅲ	Ⅲ Ⅰ

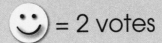 = 2 votes

Favorite Foods

Look at the results of a class survey about favorite foods. Draw smiley faces to show the data in a pictograph. Look at the key to see how many votes each smiley face stands for.

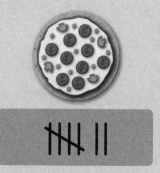

| ||| || | |||| | ||| |

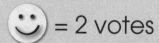 = 2 votes

Ice Cream Flavors

Look at the bar graph to see the how many scoops of each ice cream flavor a shop sold in one day. Record the data by making tally marks in the matching colored scoops.

Ice Cream Sales for June 18

© Carson-Dellosa
CD-704463

Ice Cream Flavors

Look at the bar graph to see the how many scoops of each ice cream flavor a shop sold in one day. Record the data by making tally marks in the matching colored scoops.

Ice Cream Sales for July 8

24 Hours a Day

Maria graphed how her pet Fluffy spent each hour for one day. Use the information from the circle graph to write the number of hours Fluffy spent doing each activity.

How Fluffy Spent Her Day

Activity	Hours
Sleeping	
Eating	
Playing	
Digging	
Cuddling	
Scratching	

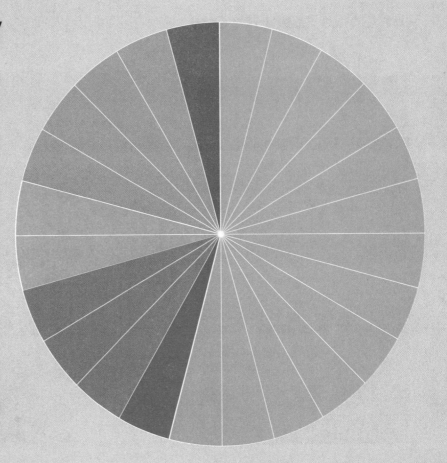

Thinking Kids™ Math
Grade 2

© Carson-Dellosa
CD-704463

24 Hours a Day

Angela graphed how her pet Spike spent each hour for one day. Use the information from the circle graph to write the number of hours Spike spent doing each activity.

How Spike Spent His Day

Activity	Hours
Sleeping	
Eating	
Playing	
Digging	
Cuddling	
Scratching	

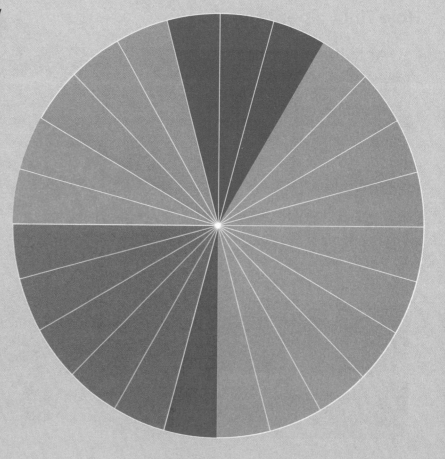

Thinking Kids™ Math
Grade 2

© Carson-Dellosa
CD-704463

Snow Day!

Use the graph of snowfall amounts to answer each question.

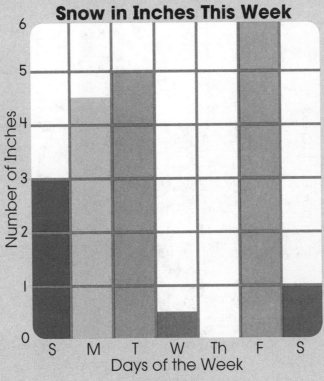

Snow in Inches This Week

Days of the Week

Number of Inches

How many total inches of snow fell this week?

_____

Which two days together have a snowfall total of 8 inches?

_____

_____

How many more inches did it snow on Friday than on Monday?

_____

Write a true statement about the snowfall data based on the graph.

_____

_____

Use the graph of rainfall amounts to answer each question.

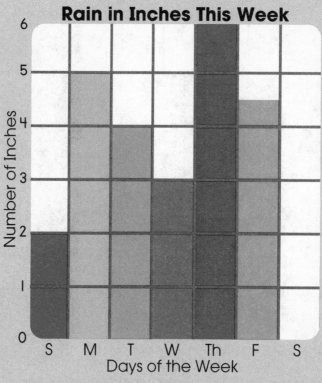

Rain in Inches This Week

How many total inches of rain fell this week?

_____

Which two days together have a rainfall total of 11 inches?

_____

_____

How many more inches did it rain on Monday than on Sunday?

_____

Write a true statement about the rainfall data based on the graph.

_____

_____

Think about the probability of each statement. Circle more likely or less likely after each statement.

With one penny:

You will flip a heads.

more likely   **less likely**

You will flip a tails.

more likely   **less likely**

You will flip the coin on its edge.

more likely   **less likely**

Could You?

Think about the probability of each statement. Circle more likely or less likely after each statement.

With two dice:

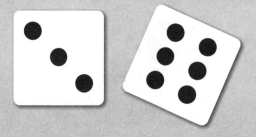

You will roll a 6.

more likely   **less likely**

You will roll a 12.

more likely   **less likely**

You will roll a 7.

more likely   **less likely**

Fair Game

Make a spinner with a pencil and a paper clip. Spin it 20 times. Write the winner's name for each spin in the correct chart.

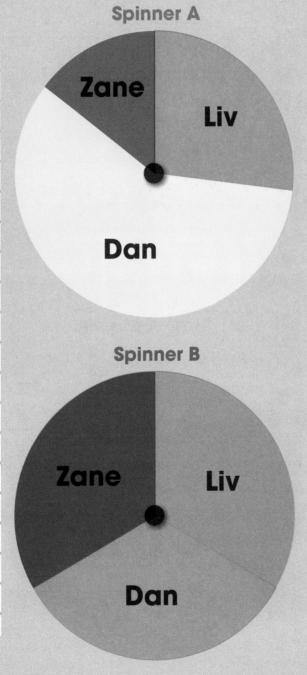

Spin	Winner
1	
2	
3	
4	
5	
6	
7	
8	
9	
10	
11	
12	
13	
14	
15	
16	
17	
18	
19	
20	

Spin	Winner
1	
2	
3	
4	
5	
6	
7	
8	
9	
10	
11	
12	
13	
14	
15	
16	
17	
18	
19	
20	

Thinking Kids™ Math
Grade 2

Answer the questions based on the spinners shown below.

Spinner A

Spinner B

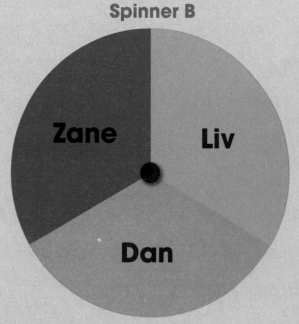

What makes a spinner fair? Which spinner is fair?

_____

What color is the first spinner most likely to land on? Why?

_____

Is it likely that Zane will win with Spinner A? Why or why not?

_____

What color are you most likely to land on with Spinner B?

_____

_____

Is it likely that Liv will win with Spinner B? Why or why not?

_____

_____

_____

It's in the Bag

Put 2 red counters, 5 blue counters, and 1 yellow counter in a bag.

Close your eyes and pull a counter out of the bag. Open your eyes and look at the counter. Make a tally mark in the correct column to show which color you pulled. Repeat this 10 times.

Answer Key

Grab Bag

Estimate the number of counters you can pick up with one hand. Write your guess on the first line. Grab a handful of counters and put them into groups of ten. Fill in each blank. Repeat with the next bag.

Answers will vary.

Estimate: _____   Estimate: _____

I have _____ groups of   I have _____ groups of
ten and _____ left over.   ten and _____ left over.

I have _____ total counters.   I have _____ total counters.

Thinking Kids' Math
Grade 2   © Carson-Dellosa
                           CD-704463
5

Keeping Score

In the first row, count the balls and make tally marks for each team's goals. In the second row, count the tally marks and write scores for each game.

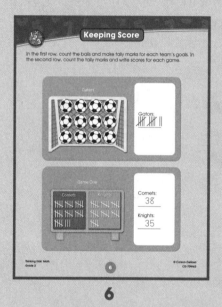

Gators: ЖЖ ЖЖ ||

Game One
Comets: 38
Knights: 35

Thinking Kids' Math
Grade 2   © Carson-Dellosa
                           CD-704463
6

Keeping Score

In the first row, count the balls and make tally marks for each team's goals. In the second row, count the tally marks and write scores for each game.

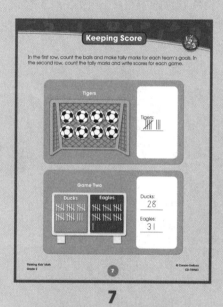

Tigers: ЖЖ |||

Game Two
Ducks: 28
Eagles: 31

Thinking Kids' Math
Grade 2   © Carson-Dellosa
                           CD-704463
7

A Number of Ways

Use base ten blocks to show each number. Draw a picture of the blocks and write the number of tens and ones in the blanks.

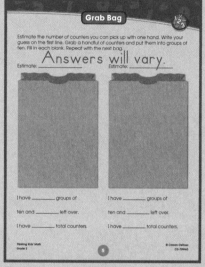

39   42

| tens | ones | tens | ones |

3 tens 9 ones   4 tens 2 ones

Thinking Kids' Math
Grade 2   © Carson-Dellosa
                           CD-704463
8

A Number of Ways

Use base ten blocks to show each number. Draw a picture of the blocks and write the number of tens and ones in the blanks.

37   24

| tens | ones | tens | ones |

3 tens 7 ones   2 tens 4 ones

Thinking Kids' Math
Grade 2   © Carson-Dellosa
                           CD-704463
9

Expanding Numbers

Build each number with base ten blocks. Then, write each number in expanded form. The first one has been done for you.

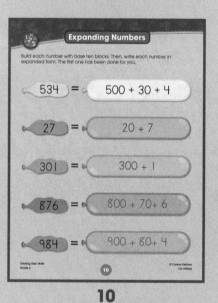

534 = 500 + 30 + 4

27 = 20 + 7

301 = 300 + 1

876 = 800 + 70 + 6

984 = 900 + 80 + 4

Thinking Kids' Math
Grade 2   © Carson-Dellosa
                           CD-704463
10

Answer Key

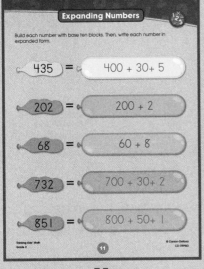

Expanding Numbers

Build each number with base ten blocks. Then, write each number in expanded form.

435 = 400 + 30 + 5

202 = 200 + 2

68 = 60 + 8

732 = 700 + 30 + 2

851 = 800 + 50 + 1

11

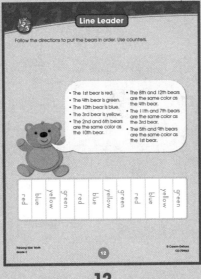

Line Leader

Follow the directions to put the bears in order. Use counters.

- The 1st bear is red.
- The 4th bear is green.
- The 10th bear is blue.
- The 3rd bear is yellow.
- The 2nd and 6th bears are the same color as the 10th bear.
- The 8th and 12th bears are the same color as the 4th bear.
- The 11th and 7th bears are the same color as the 3rd bear.
- The 5th and 9th bears are the same color as the 1st bear.

red | blue | yellow | green | red | blue | yellow | green | red | blue | yellow | green

12

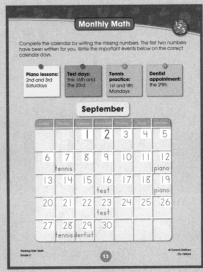

Monthly Math

Complete the calendar by writing the missing numbers. The first two numbers have been written for you. Write the important events below on the correct calendar days.

Piano lessons: 2nd and 3rd Saturdays

Test days: the 16th and the 23rd

Tennis practice: 1st and 4th Mondays

Dentist appointment: the 29th

September

Sunday	Monday	Tuesday	Wednesday	Thursday	Friday	Saturday
		1	2	3	4	5
6	7 tennis	8	9	10	11	12 piano
13	14	15	16 test	17	18	19 piano
20	21	22	23 test	24	25	26
27	28 tennis	29 dentist	30			

13

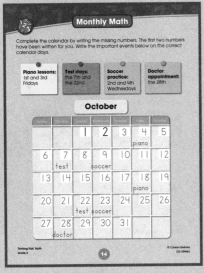

Monthly Math

Complete the calendar by writing the missing numbers. The first two numbers have been written for you. Write the important events below on the correct calendar days.

Piano lessons: 1st and 3rd Fridays

Test days: the 7th and the 22nd

Soccer practice: 2nd and 4th Wednesdays

Doctor appointment: the 28th

October

Sunday	Monday	Tuesday	Wednesday	Thursday	Friday	Saturday
		1	2	3	4 piano	5
6	7 test	8	9 soccer	10	11	12
13	14	15	16	17	18 piano	19
20	21	22 test	23 soccer	24	25	26
27	28 doctor	29	30	31		

14

Money Jars

Look at the amount of money in each jar. Draw three different bill and/or coin combinations for each amount.

Answers will vary.

$1.23

$0.78

$2.17

15

Money Jars

Look at the amount of money in each jar. Draw three different bill and/or coin combinations for each amount.

Answers will vary.

$2.33

$1.57

$0.63

16

Answer Key

Money Jars

Look at the amount of money in each jar. Draw three different bill and/or coin combinations for each amount.

Answers will vary.

$1.46
$0.88
$2.71

Thinking Kids' Math
Grade 2

© Carson-Dellosa
CD-704463

17

Unlock the Code

Follow the clues to figure out the code number for each lock.

My ones digit is 6. My tens digit is 1 plus my ones digit. My hundreds digit is 1 less than my ones digit. What number am I?

My ones and hundreds digits are the same. My tens digit is 2 less than my ones digit. My ones digit is 4 + 4. What number am I?

5 7 6

8 6 8

Thinking Kids' Math
Grade 2

© Carson-Dellosa
CD-704463

18

Unlock the Code

Follow the clues to figure out the code number for each lock.

My ones digit is 4. My tens digit is 1 plus my ones digit. My hundreds digit is 1 less than my ones digit. What number am I?

My hundreds digit is 6. My ones digit is half of my hundreds digit. Add my hundreds digit and ones digit together to get my tens digit. What number am I?

3 5 4

6 9 3

Thinking Kids' Math
Grade 2

© Carson-Dellosa
CD-704463

19

Number Know How

Show the number in four different ways. Use tally marks, number words, drawings, or counters.

Answers will vary.

25

Thinking Kids' Math
Grade 2

© Carson-Dellosa
CD-704463

20

Number Know How

Show the number in four different ways. Use tally marks, number words, drawings, or counters.

Answers will vary.

34

Thinking Kids' Math
Grade 2

© Carson-Dellosa
CD-704463

21

Write Me a Check!

Write the amount of each check in word form on the line.

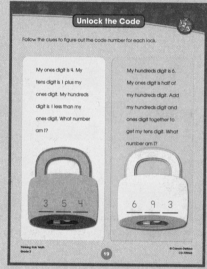

Bailey Bug
86 Spotted Highway
Insectville, IZ 3X2Q8   1001

Pay to Lady Beetle Café $718.00
Seven hundred eighteen and   00/100 dollars

For: dinner party   Bailey Bug

Lucy Love
123 Heart Road
Valentine, LU 2W5Q6   1002

Pay to Heartland Formal Wear $190.00
One hundred ninety and   00/100 dollars

For: wedding dress   Lucy Love

Thinking Kids' Math
Grade 2

© Carson-Dellosa
CD-704463

22

Answer Key

23

Write the amount of each check in word form on the line.

1003
Bill B. Ball
2 Hoop Street
Court, BB 5V8P2

Pay to Oakland Oak Trees $386.00
Three hundred eighty-six and 00/100 dollars

For: season pass   Bill B. Ball

1004
Dora Duck
314 Pond Lane
Watertown, WT 3R4T1

Pay to Goose's Pool Company $441.00
Four hundred forty-one and 00/100 dollars

For: pool water   Dora Duck

24

A Day at the Pond

Write two word problems based on the picture. Then, write a number sentence to show how each word problem is solved. Write the correct sign (+ or −) in the box.

Answers will vary.

☐ = ☐   ☐ = ☐

25

A Day at the Pond

Write two word problems based on the picture. Then, write a number sentence to show how each word problem is solved. Write the correct sign (+ or −) in the box.

Answers will vary.

☐ = ☐   ☐ = ☐

26

Fractional Flutter

Use counters to show each story. Draw a picture of each story in the box. Then, answer each question.

Four butterflies are on a bush. One is pink. The others are orange.

Three blue birds are eating at the bird feeder. Two red birds are eating at the bird feeder.

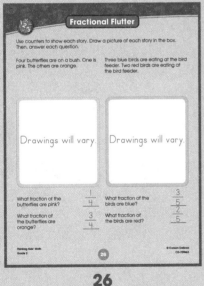

Drawings will vary.   Drawings will vary.

What fraction of the butterflies are pink? $\frac{1}{4}$

What fraction of the birds are blue? $\frac{3}{5}$

What fraction of the butterflies are orange? $\frac{3}{4}$

What fraction of the birds are red? $\frac{2}{5}$

27

Fractional Flutter

Use counters to show each story. Draw a picture of each story in the box. Then, answer each question.

Three butterflies are on a bush. One is yellow. The others are red.

Two blue birds are eating at the bird feeder. Three green birds are eating at the bird feeder.

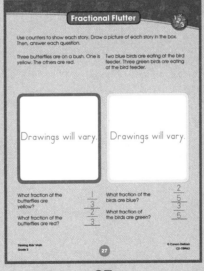

Drawings will vary.   Drawings will vary.

What fraction of the butterflies are yellow? $\frac{1}{3}$

What fraction of the birds are blue? $\frac{2}{5}$

What fraction of the butterflies are red? $\frac{2}{3}$

What fraction of the birds are green? $\frac{3}{5}$

28

Pizza Pieces

Draw lines to divide the pizzas into equal slices to serve groups of 2, 3, and 4 people. Then, answer the questions.

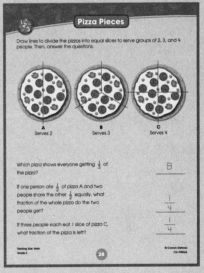

Serves 2   Serves 3   Serves 4
A   B   C

Which pizza shows everyone getting $\frac{1}{3}$ of the pizza?   B

If one person ate $\frac{1}{2}$ of pizza A and two people share the other $\frac{1}{2}$ equally, what fraction of the whole pizza do the two people get? $\frac{1}{4}$

If three people each eat 1 slice of pizza C, what fraction of the pizza is left? $\frac{1}{4}$

Answer Key

Pizza Pieces

Draw lines to divide the pizzas into equal slices to serve groups of 6 and 8 people. Then, answer the questions.

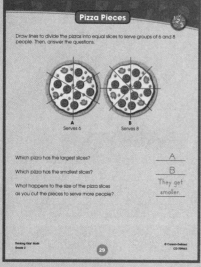

A
Serves 6

B
Serves 8

Which pizza has the largest slices? __A__

Which pizza has the smallest slices? __B__

What happens to the size of the pizza slices as you cut the pieces to serve more people? __They get smaller.__

29

Make 10!

Drop 10 counters onto the hand. Count how many of each color you see. Write the numbers in the number sentences. Repeat until you make 6 different combinations that equal 10.

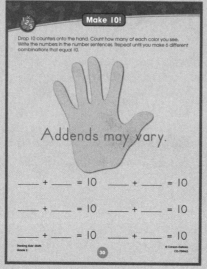

Addends may vary.

___ + ___ = 10   ___ + ___ = 10

___ + ___ = 10   ___ + ___ = 10

___ + ___ = 10   ___ + ___ = 10

30

Make 20!

Drop 20 counters onto the hand. Count how many of each color you see. Write the numbers in the number sentences. Repeat until you make 6 different combinations that equal 20.

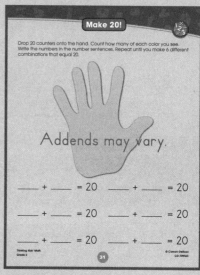

Addends may vary.

___ + ___ = 20   ___ + ___ = 20

___ + ___ = 20   ___ + ___ = 20

___ + ___ = 20   ___ + ___ = 20

31

Find the 10s

Circle the two numbers in each row that equal 10. Then, write the third number in the number sentence with 10 and solve for the sum. The first one has been done for you.

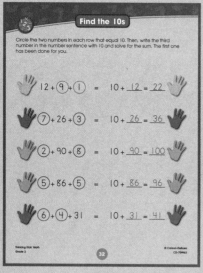

12 + ⑨ + ① = 10 + _12_ = _22_

⑦ + 26 + ③ = 10 + _26_ = _36_

② + 90 + ⑧ = 10 + _90_ = _100_

⑤ + 86 + ⑤ = 10 + _86_ = _96_

⑥ + ④ + 31 = 10 + _31_ = _41_

32

Find the 20s

Circle the two numbers in each row that equal 20. Then, write the third number in the number sentence with 20 and solve for the sum. The first one has been done for you.

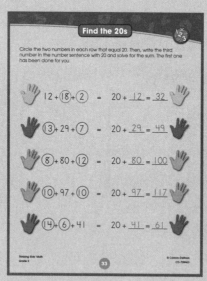

12 + ⑱ + ② = 20 + _12_ = _32_

⑬ + 29 + ⑦ = 20 + _29_ = _49_

⑧ + 80 + ⑫ = 20 + _80_ = _100_

⑩ + 97 + ⑩ = 20 + _97_ = _117_

⑭ + ⑥ + 41 = 20 + _41_ = _61_

33

Addition Breakdown

Add each pair of numbers by breaking the second number into tens and ones. Then, add the groups of ten and add the ones. The first two have been started for you.

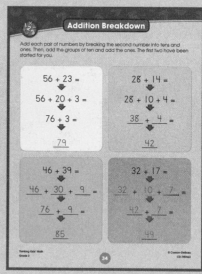

56 + 23 =
↓
56 + 20 + 3 =
↓
76 + 3 =
↓
_79_

28 + 14 =
↓
28 + 10 + 4 =
↓
_38_ + _4_ =
↓
_42_

46 + 39 =
↓
_46_ + _30_ + _9_ =
↓
_76_ + _9_ =
↓
_85_

32 + 17 =
↓
_32_ + _10_ + _7_ =
↓
_42_ + _7_ =
↓
_49_

34

Thinking Kids™ Math
Grade 2

170

© Carson-Dellosa
CD-704463

Answer Key

Page 35 — Addition Breakdown

Add each pair of numbers by breaking the second number into tens and ones. Then, add the groups of ten and add the ones. The first two have been started for you.

57 + 33 =
57 + 30 + 3 =
87 + 3 =
90

25 + 13 =
25 + 10 + 3 =
35 + 3 =
38

48 + 34 =
48 + 30 + 4 =
78 + 4 =
82

37 + 18 =
37 + 10 + 8 =
47 + 8 =
55

35

Page 36 — Mystery Numbers

Use counters to help you find the missing number behind each magnifying lens. Write a number sentence to solve for the missing number. Then, write the answer.

77 − ◯ = 70
77 − 70 = 7
= 7

29 − ◯ = 17
29 − 17 = 12
= 12

36

Page 37 — Mystery Numbers

Use counters to help you find the missing number behind each magnifying lens. Write a number sentence to solve for the missing number. Then, write the answer.

21 − ◯ = 10
21 − 10 = 11
= 11

37 − ◯ = 15
37 − 15 = 22
= 22

37

Page 38 — Square Subtraction

Use the hundred board to solve each problem. Circle the first number in the problem on the board. Then, draw a path on the board as you count back to subtract the second number. Draw a triangle around the answer. Write the answer to complete the number sentence.

22 − 11 = **11**   67 − 14 = **53**   36 − 9 = **27**
88 − 12 = **76**   94 − 5 = **89**   51 − 12 = **39**

(hundred board 1–100)

38

Page 39 — Square Subtraction

Use the hundred board to solve each problem. Circle the first number in the problem on the board. Then, draw a path on the board as you count back to subtract the second number. Draw a triangle around the answer. Write the answer to complete the number sentence.

31 − 10 = **21**   57 − 13 = **44**   19 − 8 = **11**
77 − 12 = **65**   99 − 6 = **93**   88 − 10 = **77**

(hundred board 1–100)

39

Page 40 — Dip into Dominoes

Count the dots on each side of each domino. Then, write the related facts for each domino.

2 + 4 = 6
4 + 2 = 6
6 − 2 = 4
6 − 4 = 2

5 + 3 = 8
3 + 5 = 8
8 − 3 = 5
8 − 5 = 3

40

Thinking Kids™ Math
Grade 2

171

© Carson-Dellosa
CD-704463

Answer Key

41

Dip into Dominoes

Count the dots on each side of each domino. Then, write the related facts for each domino.

$3 + 4 = 7$

$4 + 3 = 7$

$7 - 3 = 4$

$7 - 4 = 2$

$5 + 6 = 11$

$6 + 5 = 11$

$11 - 5 = 6$

$11 - 6 = 5$

41

41

42

Elevator Operator

Look at the first and last numbers in each number sentence. Did the first number go up or down to become the last number? Circle the correct elevator button beside the number sentence. Write + or – in the blank to make the sentence true.

$15 + 5 = 20$

$30 - 19 = 11$

$11 + 14 = 25$

$25 + 25 = 50$

$46 - 10 = 36$

$100 - 10 = 90$

42

42

43

Elevator Operator

Look at the first and last numbers in each number sentence. Did the first number go up or down to become the last number? Circle the correct elevator button beside the number sentence. Write + or – in the blank to make the sentence true.

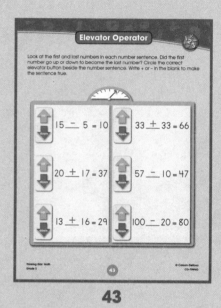

$15 - 5 = 10$

$20 + 17 = 37$

$13 + 16 = 29$

$33 + 33 = 66$

$57 - 10 = 47$

$100 - 20 = 80$

43

43

44

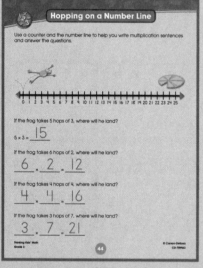

Hopping on a Number Line

Use a counter and the number line to help you write multiplication sentences and answer the questions.

If the frog takes 5 hops of 3, where will he land?

$5 \times 3 = 15$

If the frog takes 6 hops of 2, where will he land?

$6 \times 2 = 12$

If the frog takes 4 hops of 4, where will he land?

$4 \times 4 = 16$

If the frog takes 3 hops of 7, where will he land?

$3 \times 7 = 21$

44

44

45

Hopping on a Number Line

Use a counter and the number line to help you write multiplication sentences and answer the questions.

If the frog takes 5 hops of 2, where will he land?

$5 \times 2 = 10$

If the frog takes 6 hops of 3, where will he land?

$6 \times 3 = 18$

If the frog takes 3 hops of 3, where will he land?

$3 \times 3 = 9$

If the frog takes 4 hops of 6, where will he land?

$4 \times 6 = 24$

45

45

46

Fruitful Arrays

Count the fruit in each array. Write two number sentences to describe each array. In the last box, draw your own array and write two number sentences to describe it.

$4 + 4 + 4 = 12$
$3 \times 4 = 12$

$8 + 8 = 16$
$2 \times 8 = 16$

$6 + 6 + 6 = 18$
$3 \times 6 = 18$

Answers will vary.

46

46

Answer Key

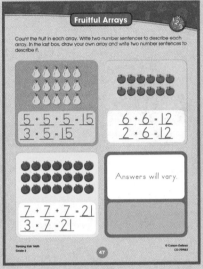

Fruitful Arrays

Count the fruit in each array. Write two number sentences to describe each array. In the last box, draw your own array and write two number sentences to describe it.

$5 + 5 + 5 = 15$
$3 \times 5 = 15$

$6 + 6 = 12$
$2 \times 6 = 12$

$7 + 7 + 7 = 21$
$3 \times 7 = 21$

Answers will vary.

Thinking Kids' Math
Grade 2
47
© Carson-Dellosa
CD-704463

47

The Great Divide

Show 4 ways that you can divide 20 counters into equal groups. Draw each way on a planet.

Answers will vary.

Thinking Kids' Math
Grade 2
48
© Carson-Dellosa
CD-704463

48

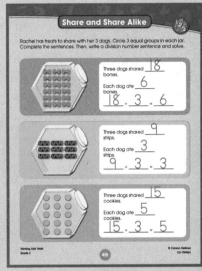

Share and Share Alike

Rachel has treats to share with her 3 dogs. Circle 3 equal groups in each jar. Complete the sentences. Then, write a division number sentence and solve.

Three dogs shared 18 bones.
Each dog ate 6 bones.
$18 \div 3 = 6$

Three dogs shared 9 strips.
Each dog ate 3 strips.
$9 \div 3 = 3$

Three dogs shared 15 cookies.
Each dog ate 5 cookies.
$15 \div 3 = 5$

Thinking Kids' Math
Grade 2
49
© Carson-Dellosa
CD-704463

49

Share and Share Alike

Jim has treats to share with his 4 dogs. Circle 4 equal groups in each jar. Complete the sentences. Then, write a division number sentence and solve.

Four dogs shared 16 bones.
Each dog ate 4 bones.
$16 \div 4 = 4$

Four dogs shared 12 strips.
Each dog ate 3 strips.
$12 \div 4 = 3$

Four dogs shared 20 cookies.
Each dog ate 5 cookies.
$20 \div 4 = 5$

Thinking Kids' Math
Grade 2
50
© Carson-Dellosa
CD-704463

50

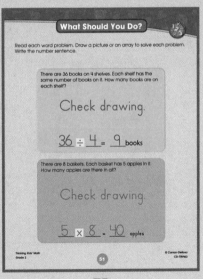

What Should You Do?

Read each word problem. Draw a picture or an array to solve each problem. Write the number sentence.

There are 36 books on 4 shelves. Each shelf has the same number of books on it. How many books are on each shelf?

Check drawing.

$36 \div 4 = 9$ books

There are 8 baskets. Each basket has 5 apples in it. How many apples are there in all?

Check drawing.

$5 \times 8 = 40$ apples

Thinking Kids' Math
Grade 2
51
© Carson-Dellosa
CD-704463

51

What Should You Do?

Read each word problem. Draw a picture or an array to solve each problem. Write the number sentence.

Logan is paying for himself and 3 friends to go to the movies. The tickets cost $7 each. How much money does he need?

Check drawing.

$3 \times 7 = \$21$

A clown at a party has 24 balloons. There are 6 children at the party. How many balloons will each child get?

Check drawing.

$24 \div 6 = 4$ balloons

Thinking Kids' Math
Grade 2
52
© Carson-Dellosa
CD-704463

52

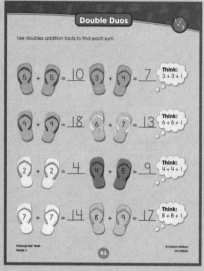

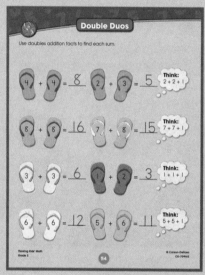

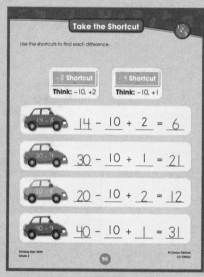

53

54

55

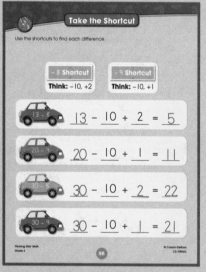

56

57

58

59

Brain Power

Use mental math to find each sum. (Hint: Make tens or multiples of 10 first.) Then, write in the cloud how you solved each problem.

Answers will vary.

$12 + 5 + 8 + 5 =$

$31 + 7 + 3 =$

$7 + 9 + 13 =$

$80 + 19 + 1 =$

60

Brain Power

Use mental math to find each sum. (Hint: Make tens or multiples of 10 first.) Then, write in the cloud how you solved each problem.

Answers will vary.

$13 + 4 + 7 + 4 =$

$41 + 8 + 2 =$

$8 + 7 + 14 =$

$70 + 18 + 3 =$

61

The Speed Machine

Use a calculator to solve each problem.

$84 + 56 = \underline{140}$

$93 - 47 = \underline{46}$

$36 + 19 + 55 = \underline{110}$

$703 - 284 = \underline{419}$

$563 + 459 = \underline{1022}$

$1,001 - 699 = \underline{302}$

62

The Speed Machine

Use a calculator to solve each problem.

$85 + 66 = \underline{151}$

$92 - 44 = \underline{136}$

$34 + 18 + 56 = \underline{108}$

$707 - 167 = \underline{874}$

$571 + 455 = \underline{1026}$

$1,010 - 688 = \underline{1698}$

63

Clothing Sort

Sort and classify the clothing into groups. Then, on a separate sheet of paper, write how you classified each group.

Answers will vary.

64

Breaking the Rules

Look at the shapes in each row. Name the sorting rule for each group. Follow the directions to show 3 shape blocks that do not fit the rule. Then, draw the shapes.

Answers will vary.

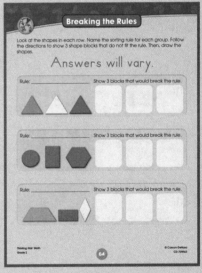

Answer Key

Bead a Pattern

Put counters on the blank beads to continue each pattern.

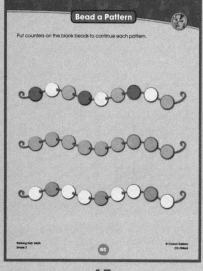

65

Bead a Pattern

Put counters on the blank beads to continue each pattern.

66

Buzzing Around

Write the missing numbers in each row of flowers.

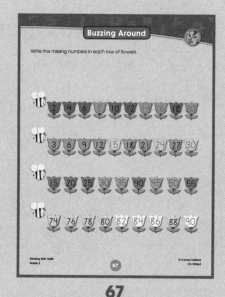

Row 1: 2 4 6 8 10 12 14 16 18 20
Row 2: 3 6 9 12 15 18 21 24 27 30
Row 3: 15 20 25 30 35 40 45 50 55
Row 4: 74 76 78 80 82 84 86 88 90

67

Buzzing Around

Write the missing numbers in each row of flowers.

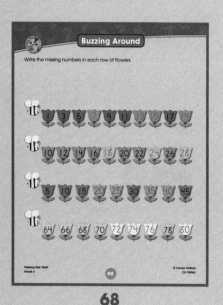

Row 1: 1 3 5 7 9 11 13 15 17 19
Row 2: 10 12 14 16 18 20 22 24 26 28
Row 3: 5 10 15 20 25 30 35 40 45
Row 4: 64 66 68 70 72 74 76 78 80

68

What Comes Next?

Draw the shape that comes next in each pattern. Tell whether the shape was slid, turned, or flipped.

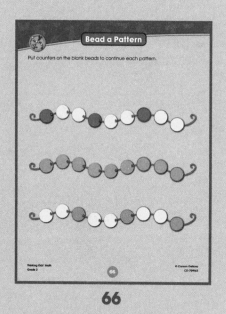

turned

flipped

flipped

69

Out of This World Patterns

Look at the rules and number patterns. Write the missing rules and numbers.

Rule: +7   7 14 21 28 35 42 49 56
Rule: -2   19 17 15 13 11 9 7 5
Rule: -3   28 25 22 19 16 13 10 7 4
Rule: -5   85 80 75 70 65 60 55 50

70

Thinking Kids™ Math
Grade 2

176

© Carson-Dellosa
CD-704463

71

Out of This World Patterns

Put a counter on each circle. Trace each circle. Look at the rules and number patterns. Write the missing rules and numbers.

Rule: +6 — 8 14 20 24 32 38 44 50
Rule: -4 — 63 59 44 31 20 16 12 8
Rule: -5 — 75 70 65 60 55 50 45 40 35
Rule: +3 — 44 47 50 53 56 59 62 65

72

Name That Pattern!

Name each pattern using letters.

A B A B B

A B C A B C

A B C D A B C D

73

Name That Pattern!

Name each pattern using letters.

A B A B A B

A B B A B B

A B C A B C A B C

74

Puppy Patterns

Name each pattern using letters. Then, use counters to copy the pattern.

A A B A A B
Answers will vary.

A B C A B C
Answers will vary.

75

Pattern Performances

Clap, snap, or tap each pattern.

Answers will vary.

76

What Repeats?

Name each pattern using letters. Circle the repeating parts in each letter pattern. Then, create a matching pattern with counters.

A B B A B B A B B
Answers will vary.

A B B A A B B A
Answers will vary.

Answer Key

77

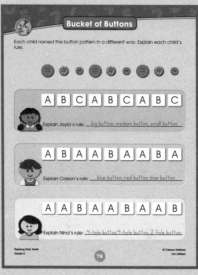

78

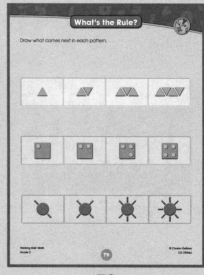

79

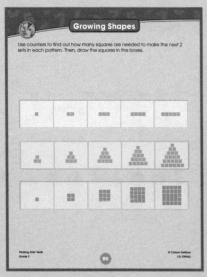

80

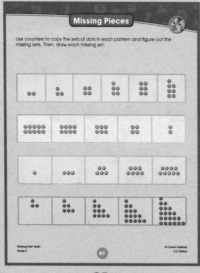

81

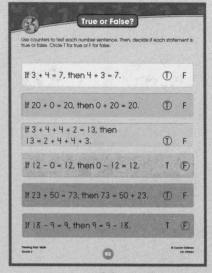

82

83

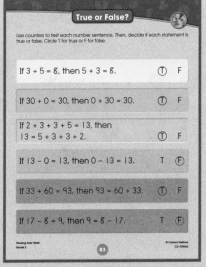

True or False?

Use counters to test each number sentence. Then, decide if each statement is true or false. Circle T for true or F for false.

If 3 + 5 = 8, then 5 + 3 = 8.	(T) F
If 30 + 0 = 30, then 0 + 30 = 30.	(T) F
If 2 + 3 + 3 + 5 = 13, then 13 = 5 + 3 + 3 + 2.	(T) F
If 13 − 0 = 13, then 0 − 13 = 13.	T (F)
If 33 + 60 = 93, then 93 = 60 + 33.	(T) F
If 17 − 8 = 9, then 9 = 8 − 17.	T (F)

84

Symbol Substitute

Use base ten blocks to figure out the missing number behind each picture. Then, write the number.

40 + ⊚ = 50   ⊚ = __10__

🍃 − 70 = 20   🍃 = __90__

10 + ★ = 30   ★ = __20__

80 − 🎈 = 20   🎈 = __60__

85

Symbol Substitute

Use base ten blocks to figure out the missing number behind each picture. Then, write the number.

30 + ⊚ = 70   ⊚ = __30__

🍃 − 60 = 30   🍃 = __90__

20 + ★ = 40   ★ = __20__

90 − 🎈 = 60   🎈 = __30__

86

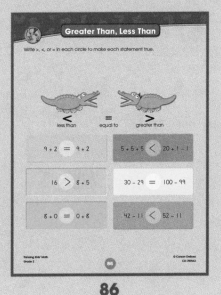

Greater Than, Less Than

Write >, <, or = in each circle to make each statement true.

less than   equal to   greater than

9 + 2 = 9 + 2

5 + 5 + 5 < 20 + 1 − 1

16 > 8 + 5

30 − 29 = 100 − 99

8 + 0 = 0 + 8

42 − 11 < 52 − 11

87

Greater Than, Less Than

Write >, <, or = in each circle to make each statement true.

less than   equal to   greater than

8 + 1 < 10 + 11

6 + 6 + 6 = 20 − 1 − 1

17 = 8 + 9

60 − 59 = 99 − 98

9 + 0 = 0 + 9

33 − 11 < 44 − 11

88

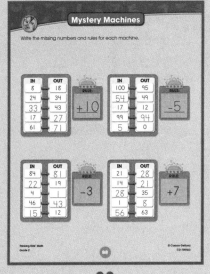

Mystery Machines

Write the missing numbers and rules for each machine.

IN	OUT
8	18
24	34
33	43
17	27
61	71

RULE: +10

IN	OUT
100	95
54	49
17	12
99	94
5	0

RULE: −5

IN	OUT
84	81
22	19
4	1
46	43
15	12

RULE: −3

IN	OUT
21	28
14	21
28	35
1	8
56	63

RULE: +7

Answer Key

89

Mystery Machines

Write the missing numbers and rules for each machine.

IN	OUT
9	17
22	30
25	33
16	24
69	77

RULE: +8

IN	OUT
100	94
33	27
41	35
67	61
6	0

RULE: –6

IN	OUT
88	86
19	17
6	4
42	40
15	13

RULE: –2

IN	OUT
31	36
83	88
57	62
1	6
18	23

RULE: +5

90

Count Up and Back

Follow the rules in each box. Write the missing number on each object.

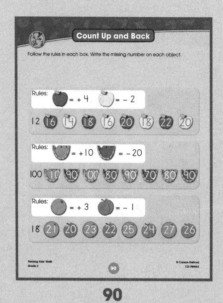

Rules: 🍎 = + 4   🍏 = – 2

12 16 14 18 16 20 18 22 20

Rules: = +10   = – 20

100 110 90 100 80 90 70 80 90

Rules: 🍎 = + 3   🍎 = – 1

18 21 20 23 22 25 24 27 26

91

Count Up and Back

Follow the rules in each box. Write the missing number on each object.

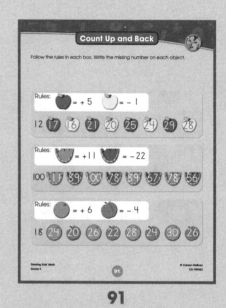

Rules: 🍎 = + 5   🍏 = – 1

12 17 16 21 20 25 24 29 28

Rules: = +11   = – 22

100 111 89 100 78 89 67 78 56

Rules: 🍎 = + 6   🍎 = – 4

18 24 20 26 22 28 24 30 26

92

What's the Weather?

Read the temperatures on Monday's weather map. Then, read the temperatures on Tuesday's weather map. Write the temperatures for each city. Then, record the difference in temperature for each city.

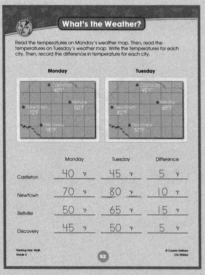

	Monday	Tuesday	Difference
Castleton	40 °F	45 °F	5 °F
Newtown	70 °F	80 °F	10 °F
Bellville	50 °F	65 °F	15 °F
Discovery	45 °F	50 °F	5 °F

93

What's the Weather?

Read the temperatures on Friday's weather map. Then, read the temperatures on Saturday's weather map. Write the temperatures for each city. Then, record the difference in temperature for each city.

	Friday	Saturday	Difference
Castleton	30 °F	33 °F	3 °F
Newtown	55 °F	58 °F	3 °F
Bellville	61 °F	47 °F	14 °F
Discovery	20 °F	15 °F	5 °F

94

Create a Shape

Use the pattern block of each shape to draw two larger figures. One example has been done for you.

Answers will vary.

Create a Shape

Use the pattern block of each shape to draw two larger figures. One example has been done for you.

Answers will vary.

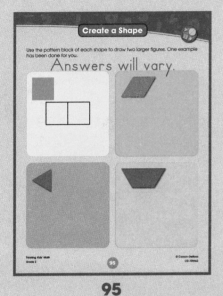

95

Shape Sorter

Look at each set of shapes. What attributes are the shapes sorted by? Use shape blocks to create a new sort. Write the attributes for the new sort and draw the shapes.

Attributes:

Attributes:

Answers will vary.

96

What Am I?

Solve each riddle. Draw and write the name of the two- or three-dimensional figure described. Write your own riddle for the last figure.

I have straight lines. I have four sides that are all equal in length. I have four right angles. What figure am I?

square

My faces are circles. I can roll and stack. What figure am I?

cylinder

Answers will vary.

square pyramid

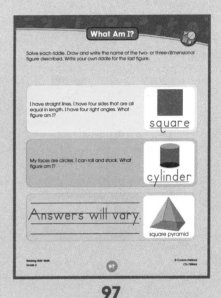

97

Name That Figure!

Circle the word that describes each object.

cube
cylinder
sphere

cone
cylinder
sphere

cone
sphere
pyramid

cube
cone
sphere

sphere
cone
rectangular prism

cube
cone
pyramid

98

The Great Shape Sort

Follow the directions.

1. Color each circle.
2. Outline each shape that has 4 sides.
3. Circle each small shape.
4. Draw an X on each square.
5. Draw a dot in each shape with 3 sides.

Check answers.

99

Angles, Faces, and Sides

Read each description. Circle the correct figure. You may circle more than one figure in each row.

six sides

two faces

no angles

six faces

three angles

100

Answer Key

Stack and Roll

Look at each figure. Decide if it will roll, stack, or do both. Circle the answer(s).

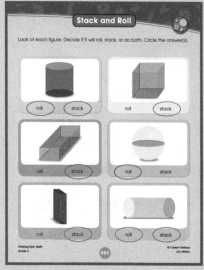

Thinking Kids' Math
Grade 2

101

© Carson-Dellosa
CD-704463

101

Tangrams

A tangram is a puzzle that has 7 pieces, or tans. Match the tans to the shapes in the yellow square. Then, rearrange the tans in the blue box and trace them to make a new picture.

Answers will vary.

What can you make?

Thinking Kids' Math
Grade 2

102

© Carson-Dellosa
CD-704463

102

Tangrams

A tangram is a puzzle that has 7 pieces, or tans.

Are any of the shapes congruent?
Similar?
What other shape can you make by putting together the 2 small triangles?

Answers will vary.

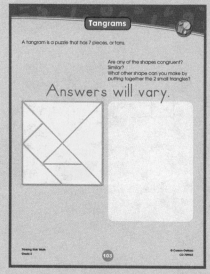

Thinking Kids' Math
Grade 2

103

© Carson-Dellosa
CD-704463

103

Create a Picture

Draw a picture using 2 hexagons, 6 triangles, 1 trapezoid, 3 squares, and 2 rhombuses.

Answers will vary.

Thinking Kids' Math
Grade 2

104

© Carson-Dellosa
CD-704463

104

Create a Picture

Look at the picture you drew on the previous page. Where is the trapezoid? What word(s) describe the trapezoid's position? Describe the picture you drew using position words such as above, beside, etc.

Answers will vary.

Thinking Kids' Math
Grade 2

105

© Carson-Dellosa
CD-704463

105

Penguin Path

Help the penguin get to the fish. On a separate sheet of paper, write the number of steps the penguin needs to take and the directions she needs to travel (north, south, east, or west).

6 steps east, 3 steps south.
6 steps west, 2 steps south, 6 steps east

Thinking Kids' Math
Grade 2

106

© Carson-Dellosa
CD-704463

106

107

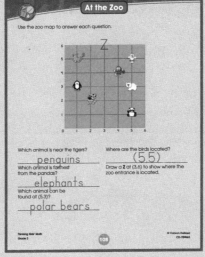

108

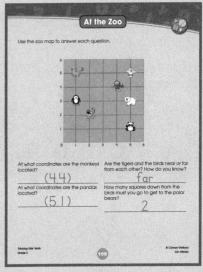

109

110

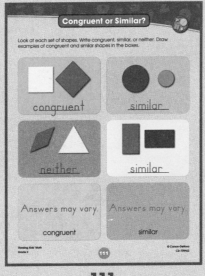

111

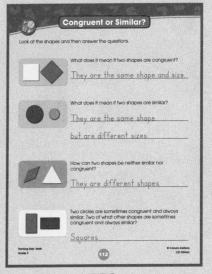

112

Answer Key

Alphabet Symmetry

Circle each letter of the alphabet that has symmetry. Draw Xs on the letters that do not have symmetry.

A B C D E F G H I J K L M N O P Q R S T U V W X Y Z

113

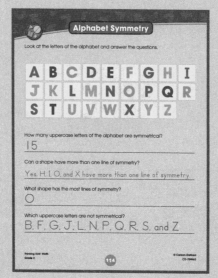

Alphabet Symmetry

Look at the letters of the alphabet and answer the questions.

A B C D E F G H I
J K L M N O P Q R
S T U V W X Y Z

How many uppercase letters of the alphabet are symmetrical?

15

Can a shape have more than one line of symmetry?

Yes. H, I, O, and X have more than one line of symmetry.

What shape has the most lines of symmetry?

O

Which uppercase letters are not symmetrical?

B, F, G, J, L, N, P, Q, R, S, and Z

114

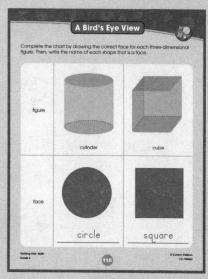

A Bird's Eye View

Complete the chart by drawing the correct face for each three-dimensional figure. Then, write the name of each shape that is a face.

| figure | cylinder | cube |
| face | circle | square |

115

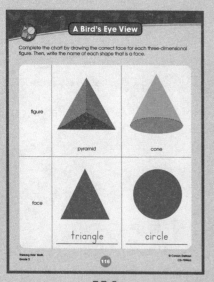

A Bird's Eye View

Complete the chart by drawing the correct face for each three-dimensional figure. Then, write the name of each shape that is a face.

| figure | pyramid | cone |
| face | triangle | circle |

116

Find the Perimeter

Look at each outlined shape. Use the length of each side to write a number sentence. Then, use the number sentence to find the perimeter.

$2 + 2 + 1 + 3 + 1 = 9$
P = 9 ft.

$8 + 5 + 12 + 5 = 30$
P = 30 cm

117

Find the Perimeter

Look at each outlined shape. Use the length of each side to write a number sentence. Then, use the number sentence to find the perimeter.

$10 + 10 + 10 + 10 = 40$
P = 40 cm

$9 + 9 + 9 = 27$
P = 27 in.

118

Answer Key

119

120

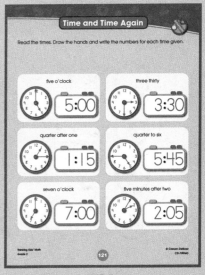

121

122

123

124

Answer Key

The Hands of Time

Write the numbers to show the time. Repeat for each clock.

3:35

5:55

11:10

12:45

125

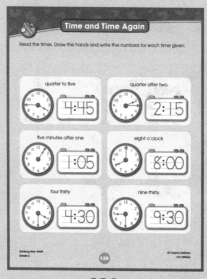

Time and Time Again

Read the times. Draw the hands and write the numbers for each time given.

quarter to five
4:45

quarter after two
2:15

five minutes after one
1:05

eight o'clock
8:00

four thirty
4:30

nine thirty
9:30

126

What Time Is It?

Look at each clock. Write the time.

1:05

12:45

3:20

9:55

6:35

127

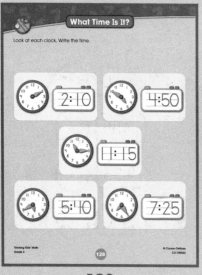

What Time Is It?

Look at each clock. Write the time.

2:10

4:50

11:15

5:10

7:25

128

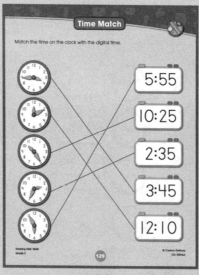

Time Match

Match the time on the clock with the digital time.

5:55

10:25

2:35

3:45

12:10

129

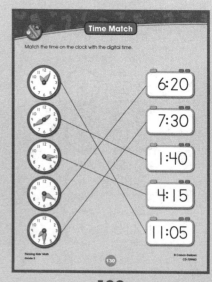

Time Match

Match the time on the clock with the digital time.

6:20

7:30

1:40

4:15

11:05

130

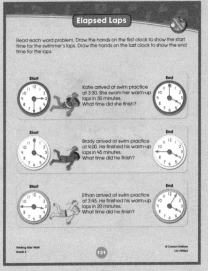

131

132

133

134

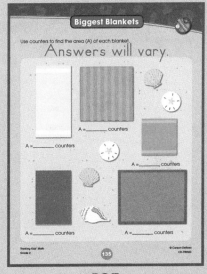

135

136

Answer Key

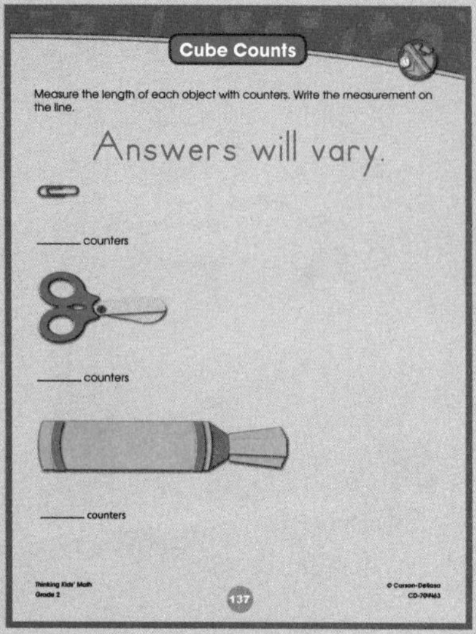
Cube Counts

Measure the length of each object with counters. Write the measurement on the line.

Answers will vary.

_____ counters

_____ counters

_____ counters

137

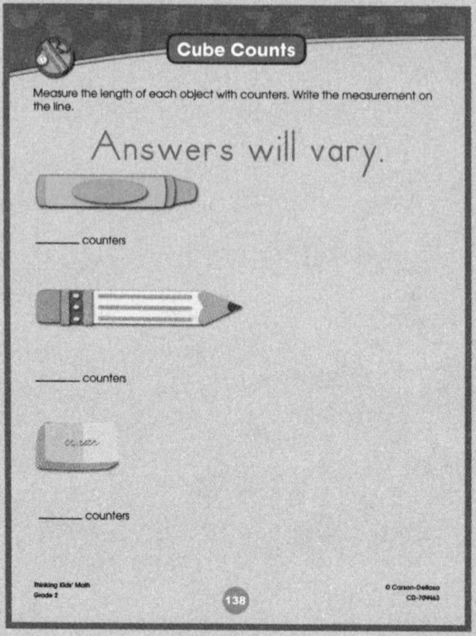
Cube Counts

Measure the length of each object with counters. Write the measurement on the line.

Answers will vary.

_____ counters

_____ counters

_____ counters

138

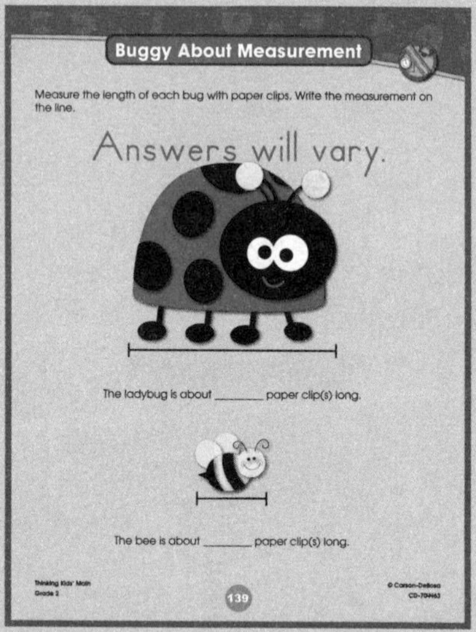
Buggy About Measurement

Measure the length of each bug with paper clips. Write the measurement on the line.

Answers will vary.

The ladybug is about _____ paper clip(s) long.

The bee is about _____ paper clip(s) long.

139

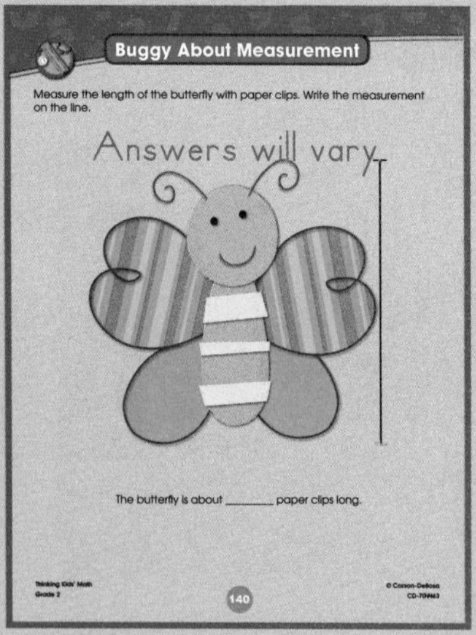
Buggy About Measurement

Measure the length of the butterfly with paper clips. Write the measurement on the line.

Answers will vary.

The butterfly is about _____ paper clips long.

140

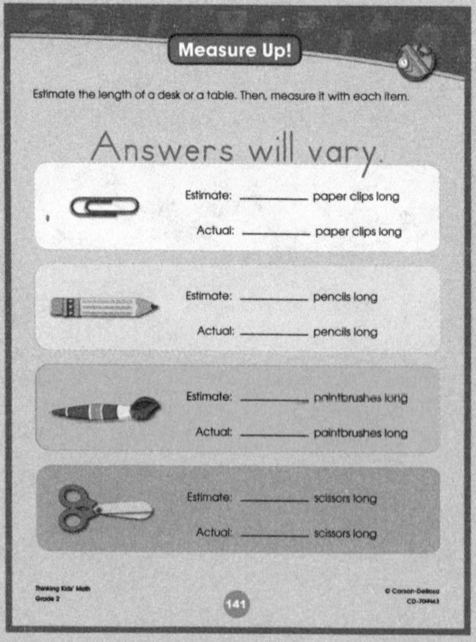
Measure Up!

Estimate the length of a desk or a table. Then, measure it with each item.

Answers will vary.

Estimate: _____ paper clips long
Actual: _____ paper clips long

Estimate: _____ pencils long
Actual: _____ pencils long

Estimate: _____ paintbrushes long
Actual: _____ paintbrushes long

Estimate: _____ scissors long
Actual: _____ scissors long

141

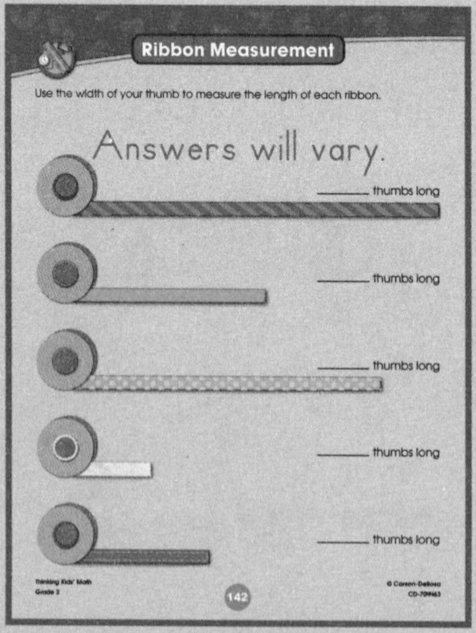
Ribbon Measurement

Use the width of your thumb to measure the length of each ribbon.

Answers will vary.

_____ thumbs long

_____ thumbs long

_____ thumbs long

_____ thumbs long

_____ thumbs long

142

143

Darling Dogs

Measure each dog with a ruler.

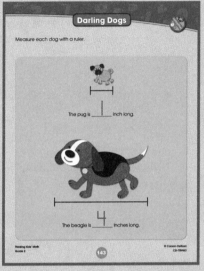

The pug is **1** inch long.

The beagle is **4** inches long.

144

Darling Dogs

Measure each dog with a ruler.

The poodle is **2** inches long.

The dachshund is **6** inches long.

145

Collecting Data

Sort a set of counters by color. Complete the tally chart to show your data. Then, answer the questions.

Answers will vary.

Color	Number

How many total counters are there? _____

Which color appears the most? _____

Which color appears the least? _____

146

Where Does It Go?

Look at the shirts. How would you sort and classify them into groups? Label each side of the Venn diagram with an attribute. Then, write each shirt number in the correct section.

Answers will vary.

_____ both _____

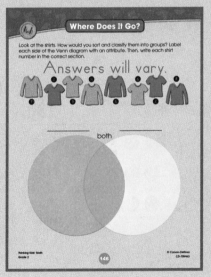

147

One for the Money

Sort a handful of coins. Arrange the pennies, nickels, dimes, and quarters on the graph to show how many of each coin you have.

Answers will vary.

1¢   5¢   10¢   25¢

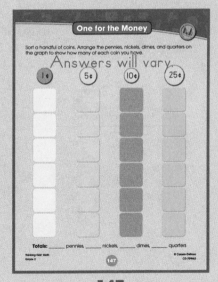

Totals: _____ pennies, _____ nickels, _____ dimes, _____ quarters

148

Pennies and Nickels

Count the coins and write the amount.

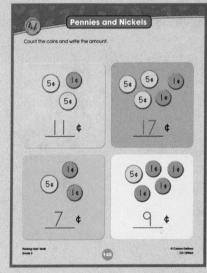

11 ¢

17 ¢

7 ¢

9 ¢

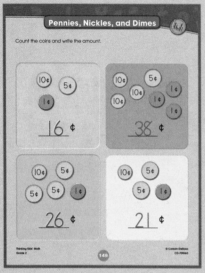

149

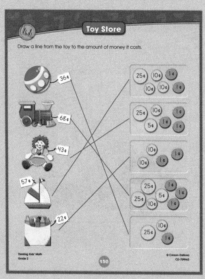

150

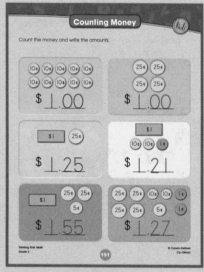

151

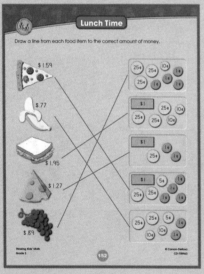

152

153

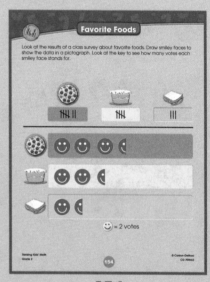

154

Answer Key

Ice Cream Flavors

Look at the bar graph to see the how many scoops of each ice cream flavor a shop sold in one day. Record the data by making tally marks in the matching colored scoops.

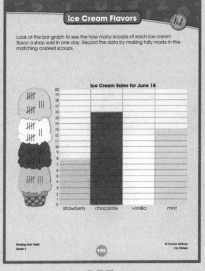

Ice Cream Sales for June 18

155

Ice Cream Flavors

Look at the bar graph to see the how many scoops of each ice cream flavor a shop sold in one day. Record the data by making tally marks in the matching colored scoops.

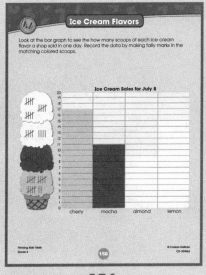

Ice Cream Sales for July 8

156

24 Hours a Day

Maria graphed how her pet Fluffy spent each hour for one day. Use the information from the circle graph to write the number of hours Fluffy spent doing each activity.

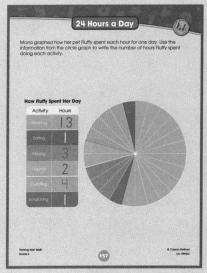

How Fluffy Spent Her Day

Activity	Hours
Sleeping	13
Eating	1
Playing	3
Digging	2
Cuddling	4
Scratching	1

157

24 Hours a Day

Angela graphed how her pet Spike spent each hour for one day. Use the information from the circle graph to write the number of hours Spike spent doing each activity.

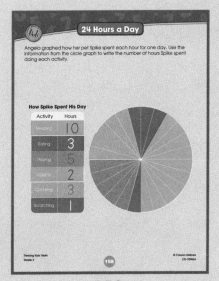

How Spike Spent His Day

Activity	Hours
Sleeping	10
Eating	3
Playing	5
Digging	2
Cuddling	3
Scratching	1

158

Snow Day!

Use the graph of snowfall amounts to answer each question.

Snow in Inches This Week

How many total inches of snow fell this week?
20

How many more inches did it snow on Friday than on Monday?
½ inches

Which two days together have a snowfall total of 8 inches?
Sunday and Tuesday

Write a true statement about the snowfall data based on the graph.
Answers will vary

159

Rainy Day!

Use the graph of rainfall amounts to answer each question.

Rain in Inches This Week

How many total inches of rain fell this week?
24½ inches

How many more inches did it rain on Monday than on Sunday?
3

Which two days together have a rainfall total of 11 inches?
Monday and Thursday

Write a true statement about the rainfall data based on the graph.
Answers will vary

160

Answer Key

Could You?

Think about the probability of each statement. Circle more likely or less likely after each statement.

With one penny:

You will flip a heads.

(more likely)   less likely

You will flip a tails.

(more likely)   less likely

You will flip the coin on its edge.

more likely   (less likely)

161

Could You?

Think about the probability of each statement. Circle more likely or less likely after each statement.

With two dice:

You will roll a 6.

(more likely)   less likely

You will roll a 12.

more likely   (less likely)

You will roll a 7.

(more likely)   less likely

162

Fair Game

Make a spinner with a pencil and a paper clip. Spin it 20 times. Write the winner's name for each spin in the correct chart.

Answers will vary.

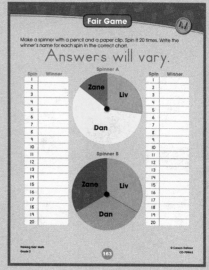

163

Fair Game

Answer the questions based on the spinners shown below.

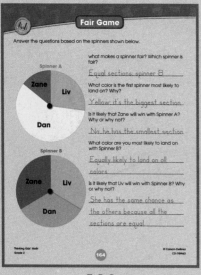

what makes a spinner fair? Which spinner is fair?

Equal sections; spinner B

What color is the first spinner most likely to land on? Why?

Yellow; it's the biggest section

Is it likely that Zane will win with Spinner A? Why or why not?

No; he has the smallest section

What color are you most likely to land on with Spinner B?

Equally likely to land on all colors

Is it likely that Liv will win with Spinner B? Why or why not?

She has the same chance as the others because all the sections are equal

164

It's in the Bag

Put 2 red counters, 5 blue counters, and 1 yellow counter in a bag.

Close your eyes and pull a counter out of the bag. Open your eyes and look at the counter. Make a tally mark in the correct column to show which color you pulled. Repeat this 10 times.

Answers will vary.

165

Thinking Kids™ Math
Grade 2

192

© Carson-Dellosa
CD-704463